What Pe
Stress

MW01269040

Melanie Smithson has written a very readable, entertaining and useful guide for stress reduction. If you're ready for easy, read this book.

— Hale Dwoskin, author, *New York Times* best seller, *The Sedona Method*

You are holding in your hands a plethora of invitations and roadmaps back to yourself. Melanie invites us to be playful with our own self-exploration and healing and gives a strong and friendly nudge out of the land of "stuck." A warmhearted and honest look at the (sometimes painful) truth: We all have blocks. It's in how we play with them that determines our ultimate creation of this life.

— Jessica Morningstar Wolf, SOMA Movement Facilitator & Artist

The Fun Starts Here! I love how Melanie approaches the challenges of life with both compassion and humor. Her blend of body, play and releasing practices makes it easy for the reader to let go of stress, even while reading. Buy the book, follow the suggestions and leave stress behind!

— Janet Bray Attwood, *New York Times* best-selling author, *The Passion Test*

Funny, warm, and powerfully accessible, this book is a pleasure to read. Who knew that increasing my happiness and well-being could be so enjoyable? Melanie isn't interested in a "do this, don't do that" book. She takes us on an excursion into the values and attitudes that underlie well-being, in a straightforward and playful way. So, when all the fun, edgy, challenging, and clearly articulated exercises do show up, we are wholeheartedly on board, ready to go for it. Melanie writes the way she lives, and she lives this work in a way that inspires us to do the same—minimizing fuss and maximizing an engaged, productive, healthy, and happy life. What a gift! Enjoy this book!

— Christine Caldwell, PhD, LPC, BC-DMT, NCC, ACS, Dean of Graduate Education, Professor, Somatic Counseling Psychology, Naropa University; author, *Getting Our Bodies Back*

If you want to learn how to release stress, this book is for you! Melanie incorporates her years as a therapist and mind-body coach and powerfully shares examples and insights that are effective in creating a life full of great relationships, happiness and peace. Take comfort in her stories and open your mind to a new way of thinking and living.

— Dina Proctor, best-selling author, *Madly Chasing Peace*

Stress Free in 30 Seconds is an insightful fun ride to happiness. Melanie Smithson's advice is powerful and engaging, and it will help steer you towards internal peace through simplicity and fun. This was such a light easy read, and her guidance was delivered through personal stories and encounters. I love Melanie's style and ease around a subject that is so prevalent in our world. Congratulations Melanie on this remarkable endeavor.

— Kim Wermuth, Executive Marketing Consultant

Stress Free in 30 Seconds sounds too good to be true, but it isn't. After reading only a few pages of Melanie Smithson's book, I found myself relaxing. I was delighted to know that I am not alone in trying to cope and find a sense of peace in this stress-filled society of ours. And I was surprised to find that there are "universal" ways in which we all become stressed. The author shares examples from her own life and consulting practice to prove the points she makes. All the good things in life come to us when we are relaxed, and humor is the great elixir to unwind the tentacles of stress. Tickling your funny bone is just what the doctor ordered—"Dr." Smithson, that is. Have fun with this book. It's a lifesaver, filled with great strategies to fill your life with more joy and greater meaning!

— Sally Huss, creator of Happy Musings, a King Features syndicated panel for newspaper; author of *The Importance of Living Happy*, and over thirty children's books, including *How the Cow Jumped Over the Moon* and *A Boat Full of Animals*

This book will be on the top of my recommended list for all my clients. I have seen firsthand the impact of stress on the body, and Melanie offers great tips and tools that will minimize the long-term effects of stress on your health and well-being. As an added bonus, the book is fun to read and you just might find yourself playing more.

— Dr. Emilia Ripoll, MD, author of *Menopause* and *Andropause*; Board Certified in Urology and Holistic Medicine

At long last! In this fast paced age we live in, many of us are aware of the effects of stress on our minds and bodies. We understand the need to let go and support our personal growth, but often don't know where or how to begin. This wonderful heartfelt guide offers that and more. I highly recommend this to anyone ready to step into the joy and ease that Melanie so clearly demonstrates is possible for everyone.

— Vanessa Morgan, LAc, Dipl Ac., Dipl Hom, Certified Sedona Method Coach

In this playful and important book, Melanie offers many strategies to alleviate stress and deal with the limiting beliefs and habits which restrict passion. Discover how easy it can be to take control of your experience of life. Warm and humorous, this book gives you the tools you need to live life stress free. And yes, it can happen in just 30 seconds.

— Patty Aubery, #1 *New York Times* best-selling author,
Chicken Soup for the Soul series and President,
Jack Canfield companies

Stress Free *in* 30 Seconds

To Chandra,
So excited to spend
a joyful, stress free year
with you!
Love,
Melanie

Stress Free *in* 30 Seconds

A Slightly Irreverent Approach to Navigating Life's Challenges

MELANIE SMITHSON

Komodia Press
Denver, Co

Stress Free in 30 Seconds: A Slightly Irreverent Approach to Navigating Life's Challenges
by Melanie Smithson

Printed in the United States of America
by Komodia Press

First Edition

LCCN: 2014900588
ISBN: 978-0-9914299-2-9

Cover and Interior design by Nick Zelinger, NZ Graphics,
www.nzgraphics.com

Illustrations by Lynniel VanBenschoten, Graphic Arts Studio
q.graphic.arts.studio@gmail.com

Author photo by Jenny Biggers, jbiggersphotography.com

Manuscript edited by Melanie Mulhall, Dragonheart,
www.DragonheartWritingandEditing.com

Contents

Foreword

Having spent most of my adult life helping people heal from childhood wounds and discover an easier way of being in the world, I am thrilled that Melanie Smithson has written about the many ways people inadvertently block happiness and how to allow for joy.

Melanie has written a guide, a manual actually, on dealing with stress, thoughts, feelings, and emotions. A plethora of tips and techniques will be found here, along with the theory to back them up. She uses scenarios from her own life, growth, and clinical practice. The book is practical, including "play breaks" to solidify her points and add the experiential to the learning. The reader will return to it again and again to glean points for action.

Melanie is a seasoned, well trained, and effective therapist and workshop leader. Her insight into how the ego works and her suggestions for distancing oneself from the ego's antics are valuable resources in these hectic and stress-filled times. I've known Melanie for over twenty years and I am delighted to see that she has used her playful spirit and approach to life to show others how to live with less stress and more passion.

In this book Melanie disassembles the idea of stress, breaking it down into its components and deepening our understanding of its complexity, so that the challenges of life can be more manageable. She shows how to replace upsets and misery with ease, fun, and well-being.

She addresses a wide range of issues and strategies including the very important one of facing emotions and allowing them to move through you, rather than denying, suppressing, or automatically acting them out. She goes on to address preventive strategies and ends with the examples and an invitation to have your own treatment plan.

The beauty of *Stress Free in 30 Seconds* is in its practicality and ease of use. You will find yourself getting caught in Melanie's creative journey towards relieving stress, and before long, you will be adding your own suggestions.

Judy Borich, PhD, author of
Touch and Go, The Nature of Intimacy

Acknowledgments

Many years ago I was told my only real problem was that I didn't know how blessed my life was. I am happy to say I no longer have that problem. (Let's just skip the problems that may have arisen since then.) My first shout out must go to Judy Borich and Barbara Flood for the transformation I witnessed and experienced at the Sacred Living Workshops so many years ago. Watching this work is what awoke the longing to facilitate change. Experiencing the workshops awoke deep gratitude. Today I am most grateful for the ability to feel gratitude.

My cup runneth over. This book would not have come to form without the comfort, coaxing, pushing, prodding, and validation from good friends and family. Sheila Burns held my hand from page one and sometimes gently, sometimes not so gently, helped steer and stay the course. Kim Wermuth, Dina Proctor, Jean Schoenecker, Cindy Whitmer, and Louise Dobish are the best cheerleaders and listeners anyone could ask for. And for honest and straightforward feedback, I must thank my brother, Perry Shustack, and my sister, Valerie Shustack.

Inspiration came many times through the dance with Jessica Morningstar Wolf. For her wise words and gentle guidance, I thank the spirits that brought us together. Soma provided a space where I could fall apart and come back together in new and wondrous ways. I will be forever grateful.

This book is filled with wisdom that came directly and indirectly from Judy Borich (Sacred Living Retreats), Christine

Caldwell (Naropa University) and Hale Dwoskin (The Sedona Method). I have been given the gift of great teachers and teachings handed down from great teachers. I am fortunate to be part of the legacy.

The nuts and bolts of bringing a book to form comprise a world unto itself. Melanie Mulhall, my editor, gets the credit here. As much as I may have resisted the impeccable editing, I know that the book is better for it. Having an editor that speaks my language is a special blessing. Many thanks to Melanie, as well, for the step-by-step guide to publishing.

I am very grateful to Nick Zelinger for hanging in there to produce just the right cover and for the brilliant layout. Thanks also goes to Lynneil Benschoten, my illustrator, for his abundant kindness and creativity.

And finally, thank you to my dear, dear husband, Gail Smithson, for always being the person who will love me, hold me, laugh with me, and cry with me through whatever life may bring. You are my rock, my champion, and my greatest teacher.

Introduction

Everyone I know is busy. Everyone I know is stressed. Everyone I know wants to be happy. Very few know how to be busy, stress free, and happy.

Some fifteen years ago, six months into private practice as a therapist, I woke up one morning feeling ill. I had six clients scheduled that day and because I was just building my practice, I did not want to cancel. As I sat in meditation that morning, I realized that even though I couldn't afford to cancel those clients, I also couldn't afford to push myself. If I was to make it through the day without collapsing, I needed to rest as I worked.

Resting meant taking more breaths, not forcing the process, not overthinking. I knew from my psychotherapy training that I needed to use the fundamental action of yielding. From Body-Mind Psychotherapy®, yielding is defined as "a quality of resting in contact with the environment and underlies our basic relationship to the world. It is about the state of being versus doing, and forms the basis for the ability to act effectively in the world."[1]

That day when I felt sick and chose to work anyway, I knew I had to yield. That day became a turning point for me. Not only did I not collapse at the end of it, I had the best day of therapeutic practice ever. My willingness to yield moved me from trying to figure out what I was going to do in the session to allowing me to be present with whatever arose. Because my clients felt no angst from me, they were automatically more relaxed and able to work with their issues. I was able to authentically respond to them and allow wisdom to flow.

This was not a brand new concept for me. My training at Naropa University included the skills of observing, allowing, and following intuition. But up until that day, I had struggled with interference from my mind, which was trying to figure out what might be the most important issue to address and what the client might think of me.

As I learned to relax with myself in session, my clients learned to relax in themselves, and the work became fun. Together we explored perspective, changes in posture that could affect behavior, and a continual flow of new possibilities. The work began to feel light with potential. Without fear of judgment, we could enter into wonder and curiosity.

I noticed that I was energized at the end of the day. No doubt, I was on to something. I had accidentally discovered that self-care could be effortless. Not only did I avoid fatigue, illness, and burnout, my clients benefited as well.

Hand in hand with yielding came a natural tendency to not take my problems and the problems of others so seriously. Adding a spoonful of irreverence lightens the weight we carry and gives us another way to interpret experience.

I have learned that the same skills that create a great therapeutic experience also create a great living experience. My clients have also applied these skills to their lives with the same success. I have worked with nurses, executives, caretakers, business owners, lawyers, property managers, salesclerks, rich people, poor people, small people, and tall people (couldn't help myself) to the same effect. Their lives became easier as they began applying these skills.

In a nutshell, my best work happens and my life goes most smoothly when I get myself out of the way. I am referring to the self that gets in the way by being too involved with my own thoughts, feelings, habitual patterns, and concerns about others' thoughts, feelings, and habitual patterns.

There are many strategies I employ and teach to get the self out of the way. I draw largely from the fields of somatic psychotherapy and play therapy, using the wisdom of the body for self-care. I also incorporate many techniques and concepts from The Sedona Method™.

Some of the strategies in this book are in the moment, what I call the 30 seconds or less tactics (or Daily Living Strategies). Other strategies are lifestyle choices and behaviors that result in needing the in-the-moment strategies less often. These can be thought of as preventive strategies.

Ultimately, all the suggestions aim to do the same thing: connect you with the love and the wisdom that reside in you. As you learn to go below the surface where all the chatter lives, you will discover the peace that is always available.

Perhaps your life is too full, you often feel overwhelmed, or you sometimes become reactive. Maybe you simply want your life to flow more easily. When you start applying the techniques and exercises in this book, your life will get easier. But reading about them won't make your life easier. The bottom line is that nobody can do the personal work for you. As you read, I suggest that you pause to do the exercises and contemplate your own experience with the topic at hand. Take notes, put reminders to yourself where you can see them, and earmark or copy the pages that speak loudly to you. And most of all, have fun! Enjoy the ride.

Part I
Daily Living Strategies

1

The Trouble Begins with Thinking

One of the most common statements I hear in my therapy practice is, "I can't figure out why I feel this way." As soon as I hear that phrase, my mind jumps in and says, *Oh, let me help; we can figure it out together*. And just like that, I can get caught in the spin of the mind. The mind loves to figure things out. It likes to be the hero. It leaps with excitement at the opportunity to solve the problem, anticipating the touchdown celebration dance soon to come.

Unfortunately, when it comes to our emotions, the mind is often at a loss. The mind's ability to filter, to analyze, and to solve puzzles is great when it comes to math problems. But it's pretty useless when it comes to feelings. In addition to jumping in where it's ineffectual, the mind often jumps in with commentary that can be damaging, counterproductive, and stress-inducing.

It's no wonder we all have a love/hate relationship with the mind. Maybe the following excerpt from my journal will resonate with you.

A Conversation with the Mind

I have been actively trying to write a book for at least three years. I have come up with at least twenty titles and thirty different subjects. I have written tables of contents, draft chapters, and synopses of the book. And still I am without a book, without a title. I don't know where I'm going.

So I'm trying something different. Just for now, I'm letting the book write me. I'm forgetting everything I think I want to write about and allowing the words to just show up. What will I learn from the book? Can I give it permission to be the teacher? Can I give up wanting to control the content of the book? Can I really practice what I preach?

Perhaps. If the book continues to write itself, using my hands only as a tool, and if my mind is satisfied with what it is saying, no problem. I can let go, I can let the book be in charge, I can give up control. I can get myself out of the way. But what will happen when the book stops writing itself? What will happen when I am staring at an empty page and my fingers are motionless? I don't know for sure, but my bet is that my mind will jump in and try to be the rescuer. My mind will say, "Let me do that for you."

I'll reply, "Well, no thanks, mind. So far, you've been useless in this process. I think we should just be quiet and wait for the book to keep writing."

The mind will parry. "Well, who do you think the book is anyway? It's just me in disguise."

To that I will reply, "Of course you think that. You always think it's about you and that you're in charge."

> The mind will probably get quiet, for a moment anyway, but I will soon hear it plotting. "There must be another way in. I always find a way, I'm always in charge. I'm the one who reminds you to do things, I'm the one who thinks of all the great ideas, and I'm the one who manifests your goals."
>
> I'll stand my ground. "Really? But doesn't that also make you the one who forgets things, the one who can't settle on a book title, the one who gives up on New Year's resolutions every year?"
>
> The mind will hedge. "Well . . ." It's confused. If it takes all the credit, it also gets all the blame. What a dilemma!

The dance with my mind about writing this book portrays the trouble we can get into when we rely solely on thinking or try to avoid thinking all together. I completed the writing of this book employing the practices laid out herein. These same practices are ultimately the tools we all need to harness the power of the mind without being at its mercy.

The mind always wants to have the first say. It doesn't care about what the heart wants or what the body might be trying to tell us. Most of us believe that if we just think hard enough, we can solve any problem. The mind truly believes it has all the answers. If that were true, I'm pretty sure we would all have a lot more things figured out than we do. Minds are very sharp and creative. They come up with lots of ideas, are good at math and equations, and can even help get us centered if we think to ask. But minds can also get us into a lot of trouble.

Who Is in Charge, Anyway?

Most of us grow weary of the mind's endless chatter, but you're probably not ready to abandon your mind. It serves us well sometimes, but more often than not, it can make us just a little bit crazy—and not in a fun way. There are times we want it to be quiet, especially when we're trying to sleep or meditate, or when someone else might be saying something we want to hear. There are times when it's useful to explore deeper, beyond the mind's babble. My mother used to say to me and my siblings, "Can you guys quiet down? I can't hear myself think."

So often, we get caught in the constant chatter of the mind and miss the deeper knowing we carry within. When I started writing this book, it felt important to quiet the voices and listen to what was important, to feel into wisdom and go beyond mind. That the mind is on autopilot through most of our waking hours, running itself without direction from us, sets us up to be at its mercy. Our first step into stress free living begins with the mind.

But how do we negotiate between thinking and not thinking? We want to be able to employ the mind to help when we need it without allowing it to take over our lives. Being at the mercy of the mind's questioning, judging, and analyzing every single aspect of our lives is tiresome, to say the least. How do we live life from a place beyond thoughts and still use our minds to complete tasks, solve problems, and create opportunities? Thinking itself is not the problem. Being at the mercy of our thoughts creates undue stress, worry, and feelings of being overwhelmed. Thinking is the strongest contributing factor when it comes to stress. How we perceive any situation affects how we respond to it, internally and externally. The same comment made to different people often evokes different responses, and the same comment made to the same person can get a different reaction on different days. Some of those reactions soothe and comfort us internally, while others create friction and unrest.

If your mind is talking to you in a nonproductive way, do you have to listen? Personally, I know I don't believe half the things I think. Some thoughts just seem to hold little or no sway. Other thoughts appear to have more power. And still other thoughts only seem to have power certain days of the week. Is it hormones? The moon? Resistance?

Ah, yes, resistance. "That which we resist persists." No matter how many times we've been told this or how many times we've told others this, resistance still shows up. Credited to Carl Jung, the theory is this: That to which we give energy multiplies. And resistance is energy. When we try to hold a thought away or try to stop thinking something, the thought hangs around, gets stronger, and just won't let go. When we can remember to stop resisting and recognize the thought as just a thought, it releases on its own. We need do nothing.

According to the research of Dr. Fred Luskin of Stanford University, a human being has approximately 60,000 thoughts per day—and 90 percent of these are repetitive![2] This translates to about one thought per second during waking hours. If you stop and pay attention to your breath for thirty seconds, you can potentially eliminate thirty stress producing thoughts. When you can remember that you are not your thoughts and that 60,000 thoughts come into your awareness every day, it's easier to just notice them. You can acknowledge that just because you think a mean thought, you're not necessarily a mean person. Or you can have a momentary thought that you don't know what you're doing, then question if that is true. A pin I found many, many years ago, says, "Don't believe everything you think." Those are words to live by.

What if you could hear your thoughts and nonjudgmentally evaluate them? That sounds good, but it also sounds like a lot of work. It sounds like thinking about thinking. Even more work. Yuck! Just the thought of it probably makes you want to go back to trying to figure it out.

Stop! Wait! Too much thinking.

The Mind as Generator

The mind is like a generator that goes nonstop during waking hours, resting only when we sleep. Do we only need to sleep to give ourselves a break from the mind? The body knows how to rest without being asleep, but not the mind.

Even the most dedicated meditators I know can't seem to stop their thoughts for more than a few moments. And yet, so many of us seem to think that we should be able to stop thinking. *It's not in our control!* Thinking happens. Period. Trying to stop the thoughts doesn't work, trying to think only positive thoughts doesn't work, and resisting thoughts doesn't work. The mind is going to do what the mind does. It's going to think thoughts—some good, some bad, some positive, some negative.

What if a thought really didn't mean a thing? What if thoughts held no significance whatsoever? Our thoughts do not have to define us. When we recognize this, we can enjoy the constant rambling of the mind in the same way we are able to enjoy a young child learning a new language. For a child learning a new language, it's like playing with nonsense. And that's *talking* my language!

One of my fondest memories occurred with my nephew Nathan when he was about three years old. It was early in the morning, and we were the only ones awake in the house. He crawled into bed with me and said something silly. I started laughing. I rhymed something back to him, and his infectious giggle was launched. For about thirty minutes, we rhymed sounds with made-up words and laughed until it hurt. We knew that making sense was not necessary for fun or bonding.

In the same way Nathan and I played with words, we can play with our thoughts, making a game of them.

Mind Play

I have taught many workshops about the power of play to restore health, well-being, and vibrancy. I have also taught workshops about how play can help us have more of what we want. It's no coincidence that the same things that support health and well-being also support living a life we love. When we learn to care deeply for the self, we become aligned with our own highest good and learn to act in ways that supports success, however we define it. In those workshops, I speak about the different types of play we engage in as adults, including sports, the arts, sex, and mind puzzles. I also speak about embedding play in daily activities—making fun of yourself when you start rushing through your chores, changing your accent when making a phone call, or bouncing in your seat when you are waiting for someone.

You can play with every thought that arises as if it were an inanimate object sitting on the desk. You can imagine rolling the thought around in your head to see if it makes it to your lips. Instead of mulling it over, you are rolling it over.

30-Second Play Break

Think of a thought that has been stuck in your head for any reason. Give yourself a moment to feel what happens in your body as you "think hard." Then just stop and imagine rolling the thoughts around in your head, like a merry-go-round, and notice how your body responds.

I tested the practice above on myself. When I practiced rolling nagging thoughts around in my head, I was able to see the thoughts rolling around, swirling together. For a moment or two they chased each other like a cat and mouse. In one of my practice sessions, while I was rolling them around, I decided to see if I could bounce them up and down. I know that when I physically bounce my body, I can't hold on to a thought. So I rolled the thoughts, then bounced them . . . and they were gone.

30-Second Play Break

Think the same thoughts from the prior play break. Roll them. Now, add bouncing the thoughts to rolling them. What do you notice in your body?

Challenging the Things You Say to Yourself

In my years of practice, I've noticed some common thoughts that contribute to stress. These include the following:

1. You must have all the answers.
2. You're doing it wrong and you're going to get in trouble.
3. You have to be perfect.
4. You're never going to get it done.
5. You don't know what you're doing.
6. You have to work hard.

These messages come from the internal critic or self-moderator, and though well-intended, they are not supportive. For those who grew up hearing these same things from their caretakers, the message feels even more powerful.

But you can challenge these thoughts. Let's take them one at a time.

You Must Have All the Answers

However you spend your waking hours, whatever you do, it's easy to get caught in an expectation that you should always know what you're doing and should always have the right answer. We also have this expectation of others in our lives, especially when we're paying for their opinion.

We impose upon ourselves and others the role of know-it-all. We strive to meet the high standard; we criticize and judge when we inevitably fail. Always having all the answers is virtually impossible, and it takes a toll on the body and the psyche. Another side effect of believing you must have all the answers is the paralyzing effect it has when you don't have the answers. The mind has a very hard time with not knowing, and when it can't figure something out, it either makes something up or starts to feel lost or stuck.

Some years ago, Lizzie came to me seeking help. After years of schooling to get the education and licensing she needed to do her job as a health professional, she recognized that she hated her work. No matter how hard she tried, she just couldn't find a way to enjoy her practice. She knew she wanted to do something else, but didn't know what that was. She repeatedly told me that she felt stuck.

In Lizzie's case, her mind wasn't interfering with the care of her patients, it was interfering with self-care. It was telling her that she had to keep doing what she was doing—which wasn't working—until she knew what else to do. We played with the feeling of being stuck and with enjoying movement in her body that went along with the *I don't know what to do* thought. As Lizzie allowed herself to enjoy the movement of not knowing, it broke the paralysis she was feeling in her mind about having to have all the steps laid out before she made any move. Her body showed her that she didn't have to know the answer to be able to explore possibilities.

Shortly after the session of expressing *I don't know* through movement, she entered an online contest to be a company spokesperson. It was a step way outside the box for her. And though she didn't win the contest, she had begun the process of giving herself permission to experiment. A few months later, she created a new direction for her life and a way to help others that excited and fueled her. And she did it through play and curiosity.

In Lizzie's case, it was the thought itself that kept her stuck, not the fact that she didn't know what she would do next or how to make a change. The belief that you must have all the answers has embedded within it the capacity to create feelings of low self-esteem because nobody will ever have all the answers.

When we stay with wonder and curiosity, we don't have to know where we're going. We can experiment and see what happens.

You're Doing It Wrong and You're Going to Get in Trouble

If you were raised by a parent who was always looking for someone to blame or if you have an employer who operates this way, it's likely you are always worried about getting it right. Unfortunately, worrying about getting it right often leads to mistakes. When you are looking over your shoulder while doing something, you cannot be fully present.

The fear of getting in trouble is connected to the vicious cycle of wanting approval and trying to avoid disapproval.

Wanting external approval—approval from someone other than yourself—is a bottomless pit. If you succeed at getting it, you may feel temporarily satisfied, but you will soon need another fix. External approval validates the concept that love comes from outside of us. Like pouring water into a bottomless barrel, there will never be enough to feel full.

Tied in with the fear of getting in trouble and the desire for approval is an underlying expectation of disapproval. Sometimes the aversion to disapproval is so strong that it is paralyzing. If you've ever had an employee who hemmed and hawed over anything they were asked to do, you were probably seeing this program in action.

If the thoughts *I'm doing it wrong* or *I'm going to get in trouble* resonate with you, the first step towards breaking the cycle is to just start noticing it in action. As best you can, refrain from any judgments about yourself and just observe. You can gently engage with yourself and say, "Wow, her approval is really important to you." And then, if you can, give yourself some approval.

When we learn to let go of wanting approval, we actually start to feel better about ourselves. We free energy and allow for more spontaneous and appropriate action.

Another fun way to play with the critical voice is to simply agree with it. When the voice tells you, "You're going to mess this up, big time," just say to it, "Yes, you're right. I will." Everyone wants to be validated, including your internal voices, and when they feel validated, they move on to something else—in less than thirty seconds.

You Have to Be Perfect

The feelings of wanting to please others, wanting to make others happy, and needing to be perfect may also have seeking approval at their core. In these situations, we try harder, we try to figure out what we're doing wrong, we try something different, or we try the same thing—all to get the ever-evasive love or approval. Often, the program of trying to be perfect arose in childhood when our developmental needs were not met. A child automatically blames himself or herself when a parent is not giving them the love or attention they need. Long after the child is grown, the program lives on.

Control is another aspect of wanting things to be perfect. We live for the satisfaction of getting something just so, and when we achieve it, we feel good—for a little while. The down side is that the fix is temporary. And in the circumstances where we can't get it just so, we worry and feel bad about ourselves. Again, the first step out of this cycle is to notice when it shows up. Acknowledging the longing for perfection will also help to dispel it. Another mantra I like to work with is this: Perfect is good; done is better.

Below is the Cult of Done's manifesto "by a couple of guys who gave themselves 20 minutes to write it."[3]

> Dear Members of the Cult of Done,
>
> I present to you a manifesto of done. This was written in collaboration with Kio Stark in 20 minutes because we only had 20 minutes to get it done.

The Cult of Done Manifesto

1. There are three states of being. Not knowing, action, and completion.
2. Accept that everything is a draft. It helps to get it done.
3. There is no editing stage.
4. Pretending you know what you're doing is almost the same as knowing what you are doing, so just accept that you know what you're doing even if you don't and do it.
5. Banish procrastination. If you wait more than a week to get an idea done, abandon it.
6. The point of being done is not to finish but to get other things done.
7. Once you're done you can throw it away.
8. Laugh at perfection. It's boring and keeps you from being done.
9. People without dirty hands are wrong. Doing something makes you right.
10. Failure counts as done. So do mistakes.
11. Destruction is a variant of done.
12. If you have an idea and publish it on the internet that counts as a ghost of done.
13. Done is the engine of more.

You're Never Going to Get It Done

If it has to be perfect, it's never going to be done. But even if you don't operate from a belief that it has to be perfect, you may be in the habit of telling yourself that you are never going to get it finished in time. This internal dialogue is one of the most common precursors to stress I see. And the reality is that most of the time, it's a lie. Most of us are much more competent than we acknowledge in our self-talk, and most of the time we do get it done. When I catch myself with more to do than seems manageable, I tell myself that since I have a lot to do, it's a good thing I'm so competent.

Play Break

Stop for a moment and think about something you have been pressuring yourself about. And become your very own cheerleading squad. Tell yourself, "I'm so competent, I'll get it done. No problem," or "Way to go. You've got this." Then just see what you notice.

If, on the other hand, you know it's not going to get done, it's time to renegotiate. You may need to approach your boss and ask, "What's the highest priority?" or you may need to have this same conversation with yourself. Some years ago, I caught myself in the habit of making a very long to-do list on my days off and then getting stressed about getting it all done. Not a good plan! Now I may make the same list, but, even as I make it, I know that I'm putting too much on the list to get done in one day without feeling resentful when I go to bed. So I prioritize the list and add in play breaks. Some of it gets done; some of it doesn't. I don't feel bad about it.

You Have to Work Hard to Succeed

Maybe; maybe not. Yes, there are many case studies that appear to show a connection between hard work and success, but there are also many, many case studies that show success happening without much effort. And some even demonstrate that hard work can lead to burnout. One story I've heard about Oprah Winfrey and her partner, Graham Steadman, comes to mind. I was told that in a presentation they did together, Graham Steadman spoke about how important it was to set goals, take action, and follow through. When he was finished speaking, Oprah stood up and said, "I've never set a goal in my life." It appears that goals work for some and not setting goals works for others.

The belief that you have to work hard to succeed is a thought you can challenge. Simply ask yourself what would happen if you didn't believe that. Notice what responses come to mind and keep asking the same question of those responses. You may find you ultimately come up with answers that don't even make sense to you.

Does Work Really Have to Be Hard?

I've been told since childhood that work is important and play is trivial, but this really never sat well with me. During my preteen and teenage years, my father and I had an ongoing and playful exchange. It would begin with some silliness on my part. My father's line was, "When are you going to grow up?" or "Come on, grow up already!" said in a nonserious tone. I would respond in song, and my father would then feign exasperation.

Peter Pan was my hero. I did not want to grow up because I knew growing up meant not having any fun. Though my father still knew how to play, my mother had given it up long before my childhood. The messages I received from her were much more serious, and the older I got, the more crucial it was that I get down to the business of life. These messages were reinforced in school and in my work life. Like many others, I was left with a longing to play combined with many messages that told me, in one way or another, that I was wrong to play.

And so, wanting to be a member in good standing with society, I got down to the business of working hard and being hard at work.

The words "hard" and "work" are so fused together that it is difficult to contemplate work not needing to be hard. And that takes us back to resistance. When I think that writing or helping others is going to be hard, I don't want to do it. Sure, I can push through it, but is that how I want to go through life?

I might be the only one with that line of thinking, but I don't think so. I have worked with way too many people who can't seem to make themselves do what it takes to achieve their goals. What if we didn't have to work so hard? Is it possible that work could be effortless? That helping could be fun?

That brings up another common misperception: The opposite of hard work is laziness. When not hard at work we are goofing off, fooling around, or shucking responsibility. To be accurate, the opposite of "hard at work" is "easy at work." We do not use this expression in our society, though we may say, "He's got it easy" and devalue his work because there is less effort involved.

Work can be fun. Most of us went into our respective fields because we had passion for the field. Somewhere along the way, effort and suffering took the place of joy. My goal, besides getting things done, is to have fun doing those things. And I also want to have fun with life. Sometimes that means not listening to everything I think.

Miscellaneous Unsupportive Thoughts

When dealing with any intrusive thought, stop and ask, "Is this thought helpful?" If it is, great. Use it in your service. Use it in service to others. If not, see if you can just drop it, or at least set it aside. Without replacing it with another thought, simply notice that you don't have to believe it.

Use the techniques suggested above with other thoughts. Bounce them, roll them, challenge them, validate them. What all the techniques have in common is this: You have to be conscious of the thoughts to use them. As soon as you become conscious of a thought, its power over you begins to dissolve.

When you begin to question thoughts as they arise, you will get more distance from them. You will break the identification with old beliefs and have the freedom to choose new thoughts and new beliefs. The need for this practice will likely continue throughout your entire life, but you will get so good at it, you won't even need thirty seconds.

2

Hooked on a Feeling

Okay, so maybe we don't have to listen to everything we think, but we still have feelings to deal with. These feelings can be even more insistent than thoughts and can show up at the most inconvenient times. For instance, in the middle of your own family crisis, your client's complaints may seem trivial to you. Or maybe you just met the man or woman of your dreams and the serotonin rushing through your body won't let you concentrate on anything else.

It is impossible to go through life and not encounter the emotions of others. In fact, dealing with other people's emotions is part of being human, whether you are a licensed helping professional or not. But at the same time our own emotions need tending to. It would be convenient to ask our emotions to wait their turn, but they don't operate that way. The good news is that feelings move very quickly when we let go of judgment, fear, and resistance, often in thirty seconds or less.

For most of us, from primary school through college, our education is completely devoid of instruction on how to handle our own feelings. It is a job left to parents or caretakers, and one that most are poorly equipped to handle because they never received any training on it either.

In the groups I facilitate, when I ask for input from participants about how they handle feelings, the most common response I get is that they stuff them or try to make them go away. We can take credit for how creative we are at pushing feelings away. All of our addictive behaviors, such as drinking, overeating, drugging, playing computer games for hours, exercising excessively, and watching television, help to put our feelings out of awareness—for a while. One addiction we don't recognize is thinking. Trying to figure out why we are having a feeling is another way of avoiding the feeling because when we do this, we are moving into thinking and away from experiencing. We also deny that we are feeling a certain way, project those feelings onto others, and pretend, even to ourselves, that we are fine.

On the other side of the spectrum, we lash out at others, cry when anyone looks at us, and live at the mercy of our feelings, sometimes wallowing in them and making them more important than anything and everything else.

Neither of these strategies is effective for truly moving through a feeling. Before going any further with this train of thought, let me define what a feeling is and how it differs from an emotion, as well as the role thoughts play with feelings and emotions.

What Is a Feeling?

A feeling is a sensory experience in the body that results from an internal or external stimulus. When a blanket is placed over me, I feel warm. When I sit in my seat, I feel contact with the furniture. And when I write for long periods, I may feel my lower back begin to ache because I've been slouching. At any moment, I can get in touch with the sensations of breath coming in and going out of my body. I may also have a sensory response to my husband's actions, feeling a quickening of my heartbeat if he brings home a gift or experiencing a nervous contraction in my stomach if he is not home when expected. And my dog can evoke a sensory reaction with a switch of her tail or a whimper in the night. We also have sensory responses to the things we hear on the news, the phone ringing in the middle of the night, and what we see on a movie screen.

These sensory responses seem to arise without thinking. They may be connected to a thought. In the examples about my husband, there is an underlying belief that if he brings me a present, it will be good and that if he is not home on time, something is wrong. But the feelings come up faster than the cognition and cannot be easily dismissed by changing the thought.

What Is an Emotion?

Emotions are defined in many different ways. The definition that works for me relates to how we perceive a feeling. For example, I may perceive a lump in my throat as an allergic reaction to the ice cream I ate the previous night or I may perceive a lump in my throat as unexpressed anger. Another way of saying this is that an emotion is a feeling or sensory experience that has been given a label by the mind. When the heart begins to race, we may label that feeling "anxiety," and when our heart feels heavy, we may label that feeling "sadness." If we remove the label, we are back to just a sensation.

So, now that I've made the distinction between feeling and emotion, know that these words are often used interchangeably, both in the world at large and in this book. By knowing there is a difference, we are able to ask ourselves if the label we have given the sensation is accurate and useful.

Thoughts and Feelings

Can we think ourselves into a feeling? Absolutely! The mind can tell us all sorts of things that create emotional responses. I remember being at a workshop almost twenty years ago and doing an initial group check-in. I was in a pretty agitated state, worried that my husband was about to be diagnosed with cancer (he wasn't). I don't even remember what was said to me, but I know that a minute later, I was feeling fine and could not even find the original fear. Judy, the facilitator, explained to me that the feeling moved quickly because I had generated it with a thought. The feeling did not originate in sensation. We can easily work ourselves into a fearful, sad, or angry state as a result of our thoughts. In these cases, when we change the thoughts, the feeling also dissipates. Many types of therapy are based on this cognitive connection.

But are all feelings created by the mind? Years ago, this was the predominant belief in the field of psychotherapy. In more recent years, with the work of Candace Pert (author of *Molecules of Emotion*) and others studying the mind-body connection, this belief is shifting. We now know there are receptor sites all over the body for emotional molecules.

One interesting note is that there is an abundance of receptor sites in the stomach. (Consider the expression "gut feelings.") This means we can have a response in the body, which we later understand to be fear or anger, before the thought comes into awareness. In these cases, changing the thought isn't going to be an option for moving through the feeling. What this also means is that unresolved feelings are held in the body. When we feel anger and push it back down, it finds a place to live in the body until we address it. Energetically, these molecules of emotion can create illness; psychologically, they can cause us to act in ways inappropriate to the situation.

You may have experienced inappropriate reactions if you've cancelled an appointment with a friend or made an offhand comment about a politician. There may be certain people you are afraid to say anything around because you don't know how they will react. Behavior that appears bizarre to others may have at its root unresolved feelings of abandonment or betrayal from childhood. You may even notice that aversions you have to certain people make no sense to you. Almost every day, I work with clients who believe they are upset about something that just happened. In truth, for many of them, what just happened stirred up an old, unresolved memory. It's easy to spot these triggers because to the rest of the world they don't appear to make sense. We like to believe we have left the past behind, but the fact is that we are carrying these unresolved feelings in our bodies with us everywhere we go.

Some believe that expressing their feelings is healthier than suppressing them. Sometimes that's true and sometimes it isn't. It is possible to scream, tremble, and cry without actually moving and releasing a feeling. You might imagine the sensation as the gateway to moving through the feeling. When we suppress, it can be compared to not coming up to the gate, and often, expressing is blowing past the gate. When we stand right at the gate and feel what is happening in the body, we may or may not feel the need to express the emotion. I have worked with those who are crying all the time, those who are angry all the time, and those who have never truly felt a feeling.

If Suppressing and Expressing Isn't Working, What Then?

If we can't talk ourselves out of a feeling, if we can't suppress it, and if yelling at a spouse doesn't work, what are we supposed to do when feelings show up?

What if you just don't feel like doing something? You may not feel like it because you have something else on your mind, you did not sleep well, or you do not like the task at hand. If you are on a deadline or it is part of your job, not feeling like it will not hold much weight. Certainly, doing it anyway (whatever it is) is one option—one you may choose most of the time. Sometimes doing it anyway is a good idea because once you begin the task, the feeling may dissipate. But what about when you *really* don't feel like working? There are days when paying bills, doing pushups, or even having a tooth pulled may seem more attractive than working. No matter how many years you have spent in training, therapy, and self-help seminars, the experience of not feeling like it still arises. Learning how to navigate this feeling is a necessary task in reducing stress and enjoying life.

But we have a wide assembly of feelings, and we must somehow move through them all. One of the critical components in moving through a feeling without suffering is to allow it to be, without resistance, without judgment, and without having to explain it. If you experience heaviness in the heart (that maybe has been labeled sadness) and can be with the sensation without trying to understand it, you may be given more information in the form of pictures, sounds, or more sensations. In this way, the body can inform the mind, and then body and mind can work together to release the feelings.

Sensations and Moving through Emotions

One day in dance class, my teacher made a comment about breath and being sensible. She didn't say much more than that, but it sure got me thinking—which is a little ironic because what she was suggesting was that we get in touch with sensation.

I find it fascinating to remember all the times my dad said to me, "Be sensible, Melanie," when the admonishment had nothing to do with the body or the senses. It had to do with being careful to think before I spoke or acted. If we truly embraced sight, sound, touch, smell, and taste before doing anything, our interactions would likely shift to a large degree.

As a society, we have a tendency to worship thinking and denigrate feelings. Many of us have been told that feelings are weak and have no place at work. Let's look at how to move through feelings so they don't sabotage our lives.

For our journey through sensations, we will follow the Nine Major Emotions as presented in *The Sedona Method* by Hale Dwoskin (2003). The emotions are listed by how much energy each contains. In other words, apathy has the least energy. Then grief, fear, lust, anger, pride, courage, and acceptance each increase in energy, with the final one, peace, having the most energy.

When we are in the lower feeling states, we feel more constricted and less apt to take action. As we move up into the higher feeling states we begin to experience more openness and willingness to engage with life. Each has an energetic signature in the body, and though we are all unique in how we experience emotion, there are definite patterns and commonalities.

Apathy

The statement, "I don't feel like it," most frequently goes with the feeling we label "apathy." This word describes what we are feeling when we don't want to get out of bed, get to the office, or do anything at all. This is the feeling that there is no way we will ever reach the finish line. So why even bother?

Apathy is the feeling of wanting to give up and of being resigned to what is. It is a sense of being powerless. When given a choice, nothing brings happiness; it all stinks. Sometimes this feeling is referred to as depression, despair, or hopelessness. Many people seek counseling or drugs to deal with it, whichever term we use.

We also use apathy as a strategy to avoid other feelings that may be uncomfortable for a host of reasons, whether they are positive or negative. One client dealing with these issues will tell me when she is having a good week, seemingly out of nowhere, depression hits. When we go back and review what was happening before the depression hit, we almost always uncover anger about an incident she has refused to acknowledge, even to herself.

I find myself in apathy when I am not sure what my next step should be, after I have gotten feedback I do not like, or when I have invested time and energy and have high expectations about an outcome that does not go the way I wanted. Apathy is a feeling I turn to when I believe I have tried everything, nothing is working, and I don't want to try anymore. I want to give up, hide, stop trying, and go live on a desert island. It is the feeling that has the least amount of energy, and many people turn to it for comfort, rather like getting in bed and pulling a blanket over your head.

When we remove the label "apathy," this feeling has a very heavy energy, and it can be challenging to lift out of it. I feel it most pronounced in my shoulders, but it permeates my whole body and I feel like I'm slumping. It's easy to get in touch with this feeling by simply moving into this posture.

Apathy will prevent you from taking action steps in your life if you don't deal with it once you're in it. Apathy can open you to negative thoughts, and you may find yourself believing things about yourself that you normally don't believe: I'm a failure. I'm not good enough. I can't do anything right. The spiral continues downwards, and we may use the word "stuck" to describe the experience. When I feel apathetic, trying to get into action feels far away and impossible to achieve.

The shortest and easiest jump to get unstuck is to feel the sensations that accompany apathy, without resistance, and then notice any grief that may be related.

Grief

Grief is next on the chart of emotions and has slightly more energy than apathy, making it the shortest jump emotionally from apathy. It is the feeling of being disappointed or abandoned, or of having your heart broken. It also encompasses pity, regret, and remorse. While we tend to think about grief as it relates to the loss of life, grief shows up whenever we think we have to give something up, when we don't get what we want, or even when we have come to completion with a project.

I remember feeling a great deal of grief about having to give up closet space when I got married, even though I was thrilled to be getting married. Whether the closet space was symbolic of independence or something else, I'm not sure. All I know is that I spent a good deal of time crying in the closest on the day I had to make space for my husband's belongings.

When we stop to notice it, we may recognize grief about unfinished projects, roads not taken, choices we made, and other aspects of life in the form of regret, disappointment, or sadness.

Since I started my private practice in psychotherapy, I have lost my mother to death, as well as two beloved pets. With my mom, there was time off to travel to the funeral and grieve, but with my dogs, Harald and Kina, life and work did not stop. And though most of my clients are kind and compassionate, when they came in for their sessions, they were still expecting me to be there for them. How did I negotiate the waves of grief that didn't seem to care that I had to work? The impulse, for sure, was to push the feelings away. Instead, I opened to the sensations and allowed myself to notice that I could expand my awareness to include my feelings, along with the client's experience. Typically, the wave of grief passed in less than thirty seconds and I became more present and available for everything in the room. This is contrary to what we think will happen if we feel our own feelings.

Grief has a similar energetic signature in my body to apathy, but it's not quite as heavy. With grief, I am more aware of my heart. Though tears don't always accompany grief, they feel close at hand.

Unacknowledged grief can become toxic in the body, and it can easily turn into anger and resentment. If we don't allow ourselves to feel grief, it can root in the subconscious and cause us to act in ways that are not in our best interest. For example, if I hadn't acknowledged the feelings of sadness about this book not being finished years ago, I might have subconsciously turned that into a belief that what I was writing about was not important or that there wasn't enough time for me to write. From there, it would have been a short step to blaming my busy life. I might have become resentful of my husband, my clients, and anything else that appeared to demand my attention.

Sometimes we even grieve prematurely, based on a belief that the future will not hold what we want. Once we fully feel the sensations of grief, it's likely that we will begin to notice other feelings, including fear, which is next on the chart of emotions.

Fear

Although fear has more energy than apathy or grief, we often use the words "gripping" or "paralyzing" when speaking of it. We can be afraid of what is happening, what isn't happening, and what we imagine will or won't happen in the future. Fear has the ability to incapacitate, and it is at the root of anxiety and panic disorders. Procrastination can be linked to fear, with the accompanying subconscious belief that if you don't do anything, you can't mess up.

Fear often shows up in the form of worry. If you are a business person or health care professional, you may be questioning whether you are doing the right thing for the client or following the rules and regulations. In a busy environment, fear might not show up until it's time to sleep. Worry, apprehension, anxiousness, insecurity, frenzy, irrational thinking, nervousness, panic, wariness, and feeling threatened all fall into the category of fear. As with all feelings, a continuum exists. We may just be experiencing a little bit of nervousness, we may be in full-blown fight-or-flight response, or we may be experiencing something in between these two extremes.

Often, we don't realize what's driving our feelings. For instance, unconscious patterns of wanting to please others, feel secure, or feel in control go unacknowledged. One of the lessons in *A Course in Miracles* (1975) is that we are never upset for the reason we think we are. We could probably enlarge this idea to: We never do anything for the reasons we think we do. When we think we know why we're doing something, the procrastination and fear doesn't make sense to our limited conscious mind, which is why trying to figure out why we feel the way we do is often not helpful. Instead we can turn to the body.

In my body, fear shows up as a buzzing or jittery energy that feels most pronounced in my stomach and arms. The expression, "the hair on my arms was standing up," comes to mind.

When we can allow ourselves to open to the sensations of fear in the body, we may find they are not unpleasant. When we can enjoy the racing of energy without resistance, we can start to have fun with it. Fritz Perls, one of the founders of somatic psychology, is often quoted as having said, "Anxiety is excitement without the breath." And, what a coincidence: the next feeling on the chart is lust, a frequent partner to excitement.

Lust

Ah, lust! Lust is fear's companion when it comes to wanting. Though lust has more energy and is more pleasant for most of us than fear, the quality of fear is right there with it. "I want it, but I don't really believe I'll ever have it" is the mantra of lust. Though often thought of with sexual connotations, the feeling of lust relates to desire in any form. The feelings of wanting more, of never having enough, of possessiveness, and of having cravings all fall into the category of lust. It's not difficult to access the feeling of lust. We can think of winning the lottery, a friend's good fortune, or any potential for having more money.

Many years ago, while I was learning how to use the Sedona Method™ to release feelings, I was in Santa Fe for training. I went into my favorite jewelry store and immediately began feeling lustful. When I recognized the feeling, named it, and felt the sensations in my body, I was able to let it go—all within thirty seconds while still in the store. What felt powerful to me was being able to purchase one necklace and one pair of earrings and walk out of the store feeling happy and satisfied with my purchases. Had I not let go of the feeling, I suspect I would have felt the way I had in the past, carrying jealousy and feelings of lack around all day.

Lust is a feeling that can arise quickly and seemingly out of nowhere. You may be going about your business and overhear a conversation about a vacation you've been longing for, or a client may even be complaining about a lack of money when you are fully aware that he or she earns three times what you do.

When I feel lust, I can still feel the jitteriness in my body that I associate with fear, but the feeling moves up and is more in my chest and even in my jaw. When you take into account the element of wanting to consume that goes with lust, it makes sense that there would be feelings around the mouth and jaw.

Sometimes we believe that lust is a necessary feeling in order to have what we want. We even lust after peace of mind and a day free of stress. I've heard many seminar leaders say, "You have to really want it," and even, "If you don't have it, it means you don't want it enough." In fact, we have turned the feeling of lust into the habit of lusting. We'll talk more about this later. The problem is that it is impossible to experience the feeling of wanting without experiencing a corresponding sense of lack.

Something I learned from a teacher a long time ago has helped me get clarity and relief around this issue. She taught me to use the term, "I have a preference for____." While this is just a little mind game or verbal trick, saying these words can help us recognize our longings for what they are—just preferences. This reminds us that we will be okay with or without the thing or experience we desire. This approach helps keep the clarity of going in that direction, but without the accompanying suffering that often goes with the feeling. We can notice that we would prefer to have peace and be stress free, but that we will be okay with or without it.

Again, when we can allow the sensations, the feeling will naturally loosen and have less control. When we take away the experience of wanting to be peaceful, we remove an extra layer of stress and often start to feel more peaceful.

Anger

At a Jack Canfield retreat some years ago (Breakthrough to Success, 2011), there was an exercise in which we were asked to think about something that we had been mad at ourselves about for some time. We were then guided through a very powerful process of forgiveness, but the first step involved yelling at ourselves for whatever it was that we were mad about. The book (and not writing it) was my topic. To say that I was surprised at the vehemence with which I let myself have it is an understatement. The way I yelled at myself for not getting the *&%$#@ book written already would have surely embarrassed me had anyone been listening.

Many of my clients are unaware of the anger they feel. But if we consider the ways we feel anger, which include feeling resentful, irritated, annoyed, argumentative, belligerent, and defiant, then we start to recognize how prevalent this feeling is in our lives. On the more intense end of the continuum we find rage, destruction, explosion, and revenge. When we get to these more dramatic aspects of anger, we find more judgment, repression, and denial.

For me, anger shows up again in the jaw, but often in the throat as well. I definitely feel tightness in my throat when I am mad at someone but afraid to say anything. Many people feel anger as tightness in the belly or chest, or even in the arms or legs.

As a side note, many doctors and scientists, such as Truman, Kubzansky, and Donadio, are now theorizing that suppressed anger is at the root of many physical ailments. A Russian medical proverb states, "Feelings that have no vent in words may make organs weep."

Anger has a lot more energy than the emotions of apathy, fear, and grief, and we often turn to it for just that reason. We'd rather feel the energy of anger than be stuck in, say, the fear of loss. Even though it may feel like we are moving in a more positive direction, if the true feeling is grief, it is important to identify that and let it go first. Emotions will move and release when you feel them, but only if you have correctly identified them. In the Jack Canfield exercise referred to above, it was easy to access the fear that was underlying the anger. When I was able to feel the fear, as well as the anger, both feelings were able to move and dissolve.

When we hold on to anger and resentment, our judgments become clouded and we can easily miss opportunities that are right in front of us.

Pride

As defined in *The Sedona Method*, pride is the feeling of being better than something or someone else. It can be a sense of aloofness or disdain, and when we are experiencing pride, we can be patronizing and judgmental. It is the feeling that arises when we dismiss someone else's work or approach to life, believing we know or can do better. (What I consider the positive aspects of pride are included in the emotion of courage.)

Like anger, many think that they are not proud, but if you think of all the "lousy drivers" and "incompetent clerks or operators," and if you contemplate all the times you wanted to show someone else how something should be done, you will easily get in touch with this feeling.

For any helping professional, it's easy to slip into judgment when a client shares a story about bad habits or poor decisions. We can also feel pride if we are given credit for positive change in a client's life, which is a slippery slope. Yes, the acknowledgment is nice, but there is a flip side. Those who will give us credit for their positive change will often blame us when there is no progress seen. Worse, if we accept responsibility for the positive change, we will probably also accept the blame if no positive change is seen.

Pride can show up when we see someone doing something we want to be doing and think we could do a better job. While this may or may not be true, it gets in the way of appreciating the other and seeing them clearly. In a lot of ways, feeling proud helps us avoid what may be below the surface, which could be anger with ourselves for not taking the actions steps we could be taking to change our own life or grief over not having been given the same opportunities.

In my body, the feeling of pride is in the chest area (think of the lion), all puffed up, but then it feels like the energy stops right around my throat and doesn't make it up into my head. It's almost as if pride doesn't let me think straight. When we are living in pride or stuck in it for the moment, we may refuse good job offers or turn down dates because we think they are beneath us. We are also likely to sabotage our own action steps, all the while feeling annoyed with the world.

Courage

Finally, we get to the "fun" or the "preferred" emotions. Forms of courage include a sense of adventure, alertness, aliveness, competency, creativeness, dynamism, spontaneity, and vision. When feeling courage, we are ready to take risks, go for it, and do whatever it takes. In courage, we may feel bombarded with new, great ideas.

Unlike the feelings that came before this, courage is an emotion we might want more of. It's a very productive state. When I am lacking in this feeling, I might remind myself that that there are people who love and support me, that I am not the first to struggle with whatever issue is up for me, and that many people have been helped by the concepts and practices I am teaching. I might also take a moment to remember the messages I want to bring to the world and my passion for doing what I am doing.

Sometimes courage can blind us to what we are doing or getting into. I've taken some huge risks in my life, oblivious to the consequences. When I moved from New York to Santa Fe, I had no idea of the emotional impact it would have on me. Many people commented on how courageous I was to make that move. My sense of adventure was the motivating factor, but reason and consequences were, to a large degree, disregarded.

Few people fail to enjoy this energy. Courage provides an adrenaline rush, and it can motivate us to start new projects and take action.

I feel energy pulsating through my entire body and a sense of urgency to get going as I tap into courage. I can also feel this emotion in my chest, but with more of a push towards action and more connection to my head than with pride.

Where this energy could potentially get us in trouble is having too many good ideas, jumping from one project to the next, and never actually completing anything. It's easy for me to go into overwhelm and then drop back into apathy if I try to make courage a permanent state.

Acceptance

Acceptance is a place of integration, of allowing all the feelings to do whatever they are doing and allowing life and others to be. In acceptance, we feel in tune, we feel loving, joyful, playful, and open. There is a sense of well-being and a knowing that all will work out as it should (even if it's not how we would design it).

When we are feeling acceptance, we are able to take action without attachment to the outcome. We are simply in a place of knowing what we need to do next. If we are faced with a challenge, we stay calm and explore options for moving through it.

People often confuse the concept of acceptance with apathy or giving up, but if you have been following the chart of emotions with me, you know the two feelings are very different in the body. In apathy, the mantra is, "I don't care; it all stinks." In acceptance, it is, "I don't mind; it's all great."

The most effective way I know to cultivate the feeling of acceptance is to feel all the emotions that get in the way of it. Too often, we try to accept a situation that we are angry about, disappointed with, or jealous of. If we allow these feelings to move through us, acceptance naturally arises. With acceptance, there is a knowing that we are ultimately not in charge, and that is okay. One of the nice things I have learned about acceptance is that it eventually becomes more of a natural state, rather than something we need to keep working at cultivating.

When I am in acceptance, I feel energy in my whole body, but it feels more contained and easier to direct than in courage. It could be said that acceptance is a freeing up of trapped energy or a release of energy. I can sit and write, make phone calls, give a great speech, enjoy my clients, and just about everything else when I am in acceptance. Even the annoying things just are. It is a highly productive place to be and, at the same time, peaceful.

Peace

I could almost leave this section blank. The state of peace is one of serenity, stillness, or tranquility. Often depicted in images as water or sky, there is a quality of being expanded or unlimited associated with peace. It is technically beyond emotion. Rather, it is a state of awareness that is unaffected, similar to a screen upon which a movie plays or the ocean upon which the waves occur.

For many of us, this state is most often accessed in meditation or on retreat. When I try to feel it in my body, what I actually notice is an awareness of my body and a sense of detachment from it, a remembering that I am more than my body, more than my thoughts, and more than my emotions. Peace arises when we recognize that we are not the emotional waves that move through us, but that which is aware of the waves.

When I think about my book in this state, I recognize that it is just a form of energy I have created many emotional stories about. These are the rational days.

Making Friends with Emotions

You have by now begun to get a sense of the impermanence of emotions, a sense that they are simply waves of energy that move through us. Sometimes we identify with the emotions and think they are attached to us; sometimes we don't. When we can just allow them to move through us, which is what happens when we don't resist them, they let go of their own accord. This is the nature of energy. It is not permanent. It is the resistance to energy that feeds it and keeps it hanging around, making us feel stuck.

The beauty of recognizing how many emotions move through us on a daily basis is that it brings with it the ability to choose how to be with them. When they are made conscious, we can decide whether to hold on to them and keep them alive or feel them and allow them to let go.

All emotions are easily accessible at any time for most of us, but many people have been taught to hide and suppress emotions at any cost. If this is the case for you, I encourage you to be gentle with yourself and do the exercises repeatedly until you can start to feel your feelings. Remember, if you don't feel them, they will hang around and sabotage you in ways you cannot determine.

A great way to get in touch with your feelings about your work or your life is to go through the chart as I did in this chapter. You can think about a specific situation or all of life as you move through the emotions. Start with apathy. Notice what thoughts show up and what you feel in your body. Then move on to grief, fear, lust, anger, pride, courage, acceptance, and peace. If it's initially challenging for you to get in touch with what you feel in your body, take a look at how I described them for me and go from there. Remember, this is just a starting place. Every body is unique, and you may feel something very different than I feel. Simply allow yourself to feel the feeling. Most feelings will naturally and easily let go when you breathe with them.

Another way to get information on what you are feeling is through art. Journaling, drawing, painting, dancing, and every other art form I can think of are great vehicles for allowing emotions to move. If you need a starting place, follow the chart of emotions from apathy to peace. What color is lust? How does grief move? What might anger say? Allow yourself to play with colors, movement, shapes, and textures without judging yourself.

A common feeling experience worth playing with is overwhelm. Overwhelm is closely linked to fear, but with accompanying beliefs that we won't ever catch up. One morning, I woke up feeling a lot of anxiety, thinking that I had double-booked myself for an appointment. When I rose and checked my schedule, I realized I hadn't, but it was close. With the hundreds of things on my list each day, sometimes it feels like there is no way I'll ever get caught up. When I imagine that, I see myself walking down the street trying to catch up with myself. "Wait, Melanie, I'm back here. How far do you think you're going to get without me?" When I turn the thought into an image, it gets comical. And instead of producing anxiety, it produces laughter.

Another way I play with the feeling of overwhelm is to imagine that I am performing the circus act of spinning plates. I let myself feel the craziness of trying to keep all the plates spinning at once, seeing myself run from one spinning stick to the next. Then I imagine letting all the plates crash to the floor simultaneously. I love the sound of crashing plates! Once the plates crash, I breathe a big sigh of relief. Now I can think straight.

And if you feel as if you are running out of time, it is helpful to remind yourself that there is really no place you need to get to. As Eckhart Tolle points out, if you could ask an eagle or a lion what time it is, they would tell you that it is now. If I can remind myself of my animal nature and be here, right now, then I can be as the lion, present to what I am doing.

When Feelings Won't Let Go

What do we do when the feeling just won't let go? Sometimes we feel nothing is going to help and we are going to be stuck with a particular feeling for a very long time. At times like these, it is particularly important to let go of resistance. Let the feeling have its way with you. Tell the fear, "Bring it on." Tell the anger, "Go ahead, explode." (Just don't explode on others!) When the feeling won't let go, at least part of the reason for it is that we are still suppressing part of it. When we allow it to become full-blown, any hidden aspects will rise to the surface. We are also addressing the fear of the feeling, whether it's fear of fear or any other feeling. When we give the feeling permission to go full-blown, we are actually stepping into courageousness, knowing that we are strong enough to take it.

If you have trouble getting in touch with your feelings, go global. Sometimes thinking about something impersonal, like politics or social issues, makes it easier to get in touch with feelings. If you can't find anything in your life that you are or could be upset about, expand beyond yourself. Let yourself feel grief about children starving, wars, natural disasters. Get in touch with anger about injustice. The important thing is to feel the feelings so they can move through and dissolve.

When we learn to allow or dance with the emotions, they no longer have the power to control us. We become free to engage with life knowing we are capable of being with the feelings that may arise. A true sense of competency develops as we learn to be with ourselves through every emotional experience. And that's the best stress reduction technique of them all.

Initially, there may be an investment of time necessary, though much of that investment is in daily awareness. Eventually, you will learn that most feelings can fully move through your body in less than thirty seconds.

3

Dealing with Habits

Let's say, for the sake of argument, that you have mastered the thoughts and feelings that create stress for you on a daily basis. Great! Now it's time to address the habitual patterns of worrying, procrastinating, lusting, overindulging, and criticizing. You may recognize that lust is here again, as is worry, which was included in the feeling of fear. It's no mistake. Sometimes we take a feeling and turn it into a repetitive behavior.

We are all guilty of engaging in at least one of these counterproductive behaviors on occasion, if not all of them, all of the time. These behaviors may even appear to be running without our permission, which speaks to the unconscious nature of these patterns. My personal definition of a habit is a repetitive pattern of behavior that often appears to happen without conscious awareness. Some habits, like brushing your teeth on a daily basis, are useful. Biting your nails? Not so much.

From a neuroscience perspective, habits may form familiar neural pathways, making them difficult, but not impossible, to change. Neural patterns get established in the corpus striatum complex (or basal ganglia), a brain region critical to habits, addiction, and procedural learning. A neural pattern gets stronger with repeated visits. Similar to walking the same path up a mountain hundreds of times, that path will be easier to follow than one you have only walked once or twice. This same area of the brain is also responsible for managing memorized movement, that is, movement we undertake without forethought. An excess of dopamine in this part of the brain is now believed to contribute to obsessive compulsive disorder (OCD), previously believed to be a psychological disorder, not a physical or brain chemistry disorder.[4] There we go again, trying to separate the body and the mind.

Think about your compulsive habits. Do you ever feel like you're a little OCD and judge and/or punish yourself for this?

We may realize that we both love and hate our habits. They can bring comfort, relief, angst, joy, guilt, and many other emotions, sometimes at the very same time. We may like some of our habits, particularly those that are not compulsive and appear to support health—habits like journaling, meditating, dancing, or working out at the gym. These I think of as deliberate habits coming from discipline and joy rather than from compulsion or reaction. But even the negative habits exist on a continuum with "bad but not terrible" on one end to "worst" at the other. Television watching and procrastination aren't as bad as worrying and overindulging (at least in my mind). Lusting and criticizing aren't bad if they come and go, but spending a whole day in lust or criticizing everything we think, do, and say moves these habits down to the "worst" end of the continuum.

How did these habits develop, anyway? Are they learned behaviors or our very own self-developed coping strategies?

Worrying

If we start by looking at the habit of worrying using my experience as a case study, it is clear that worrying is a learned behavior. I believe my mother started teaching me how to worry when I was in the womb. It wasn't her fault. I'm sure she was well taught herself in this area, and she had plenty to worry about. I was an Rh factor baby, which in the 1950s meant I was a high-risk pregnancy, and she could lose me at any time. So she worried. It's what she believed there was to do under those circumstances.

My mother's belief was contrary to everything we know about worrying, including that it's not helpful and can even make matters worse. Worry is akin to stress, which is linked to many physical ailments. Yet we defend, justify, and explain our right to worry—and sometimes believe that if we stop worrying, we will miss something.

In other words, we use worrying in place of mindfulness. We convince ourselves that we have to worry about drunk drivers or we'll get hit by one, or even become one. We don't trust ourselves to pay attention, take right action, and respond appropriately to a situation. In fact, we are reinforcing the negative self-perception that we are not capable of handling what arises, even though we are perfectly capable most of the time. When we do this, we are, in effect, planning to either forget or mess up, so we tell ourselves to worry to compensate for our shortcomings. We also use worry in place of lists, as a way to remember to pay a bill or otherwise take care of something. Why we would choose worry instead of pen and paper is beyond anything I can even fathom—but we do.

We also use the habit of worrying to induce the feeling of guilt, and then we use the guilt to push ourselves into action. In practice, it would go like this: I tell myself to remember to call Kim because she'll be mad at me if I don't. Then I worry that I will forget and worry that when I do, Kim will be mad at me. This is an example of affirming a negative belief that I am lazy or incapable of doing the things that will keep me in integrity with myself and others. I may not be consciously thinking these things, but if I am involved in this cycle of worrying, there is an underlying concern that I am unable to handle the situation.

In fact, in the field of positive psychology, worry is described as a response to a moderate challenge for which the subject has inadequate skills.[5] When we worry, we are, in effect, telling ourselves that we have inadequate skills, whether or not this is true.

As a noun, worry is a state of mind that is filled with anxiety and uncertainty over actual or potential problems. As a verb, worry is actively engaging in fearful thoughts. As a noun, worry is a feeling state on the fear continuum. But when we are worrying, it is no longer a feeling state because now we are doing something. We have taken the feeling and turned it into an activity. And as far as activities go, few are less fun or productive than worrying. When engaged in worrying, we are giving energy and attention to what we least want to have happen. In the book scenario, I was worrying that it would never get done. Think about the last time you worried. What was the picture you were holding in mind? When we worry, we hold a picture of what we don't want in consciousness. You may have heard that what you pay attention to multiplies. When we worry, we are paying attention to lack or disaster. And I'm pretty sure that is not what we want.

30-Second Play Break

Think about something that worries you. Notice what pictures you are holding in your mind when you worry. Ask yourself if you could let go of that picture. Sometimes it's easier to find a replacement picture, but it's not necessary.

Ending Worry

For years I taught workshops on the dangers of worry. And guess what? I couldn't seem to stop the worrying. Since then, I've learned some tricks that have been very helpful. (Yes, I do think we sometimes have to trick ourselves.) And now worry has dropped off my list of favorite pastimes. Just in case you ever worry, here are my tips.

Stop resisting.

As stated previously, when we resist a thought, feeling, or habit, it persists. Resistance to worrying seems to arise almost simultaneously with worrying. One part of the mind starts to imagine a bad scenario, and then another part of the mind shows up and says, "Don't worry." A battle ensues between the parts of us that urge us to worry and the parts that urge us to not worry. Most of us are familiar with this experience, and when we say things like, "I'm worried to death," or "I'm worried sick," those words can become a self-fulfilling prophecy.

To get out of the cycle created by resistance to worrying, give yourself permission to worry. Make the act of worrying conscious and deliberate. Maybe even throw yourself a worry party. At the party, take worrying to its extreme. Allow your mind to create every worst case scenario it can imagine and give yourself lots of approval for being so good at worrying.

If I was going to worry about the book never getting finished, the conversation at my party would sound something like this: "You're never going to finish the book. People will make fun of you for saying you're writing a book. Your clients will lose faith in you and leave you, and you will be forced to close your practice and go begging on the streets."

Be sure to keep going with your party until it becomes amusing or you are entertained by it. Maybe you can even enter a worry contest, confident that you will walk away the winner. If you are shuddering at the mere thought of giving yourself permission to worry, set a time limit (at least five minutes) and see what happens. You might find that it works for you. You might even feel relieved by doing it.

Turn the verb into a noun.

If you have taken the feeling of worry and turned it into something to do, then it makes sense to stop for a minute and feel the feeling. Strange as it may sound, sometimes we are so afraid to experience a feeling that we would prefer to engage in worrying.

Try turning the worry from a verb into a noun.

For instance, in relation to writing this book, "worry" as a verb would go like this: I wake up in the morning with a clenching in my chest and the thought, *When am I going to find time to write today?* That is quickly followed by another thought. *You're getting behind on your page count.* And another. *There's no time to write.* And another. *If you take the time to write, you won't get to walk the dog or go to dance class.* Now the clenching in my chest is getting tighter and my stomach is starting to hurt.

As a noun, it would go like this: I experience that clenching in my chest and ask some questions. *What's really here under the mind chatter and all the labels? A sensation, that's all. Can I allow myself to feel the sensation and breathe with it? Can I acknowledge the feeling and maybe even validate that writing a book is a little scary? Can I maybe even give myself some credit for being so brave?* I find myself starting to settle down. Now my mind gets more creative with finding time to write. Just making that little bit of space in my body to feel the sensations creates a sense of time and space in my day. Amazing.

Other examples might be worrying about what the doctor will say rather than feeling the fear of facing illness, worrying about what someone else will think rather than asking yourself what you think or feel, or worrying about your child's college choices instead of facing your own feelings about being an empty nester. We can take almost any experience and turn it into an opportunity to worry, but we can also catch ourselves in the act and make a different choice.

See what's driving it.

What do you think you will get from worrying? Love? During the first year of my marriage, my husband and I were living in Santa Fe and his young daughters were living in Albuquerque. They spent most weekends with us, which meant we were making the fifty-mile drive to get them and bring them back almost every week. I often skipped at least one of the trips. I'm sure I had something more important to do, like stay home and worry! I can't remember when I realized that my worrying was making my husband, Gail, angry. Didn't he realize that if you love someone, you worry about them? (Remember my womb experience.) Didn't he feel cherished and cared about when I worried? He was the one who caused me to worry in the first place, so why was he mad at me?

Well, as it turns out, my husband was raised in a different environment. If you trusted someone, you didn't worry about them. How odd. But somehow, this made sense to me. When we worry about someone, there is an implication that they won't be able to handle the circumstances of their life. (It also implies that our worrying will somehow make them more competent.) Is this really the message we want to send to our loved ones? Is it even what we want to think or believe about them—that they are incompetent? And I thought that worrying was an expression of love that my husband would appreciate. How wrong I was. What's really crazy about this thinking is that when we are worrying, we are caught in the energy of fear and it is impossible to feel love. If you worry because you love them, stop and just love them instead.

Do you think you will get safety from worrying? Love isn't the only feeling confused (or fused) with worry. We also think that worrying will give us the feeling of safety. In my case, that translated to believing that if I worried the whole time my husband was driving between Santa Fe and Albuquerque, he would be safe. On the other hand, if I was out having a good time while he was gone, I was somehow dropping the ball or not doing my job.

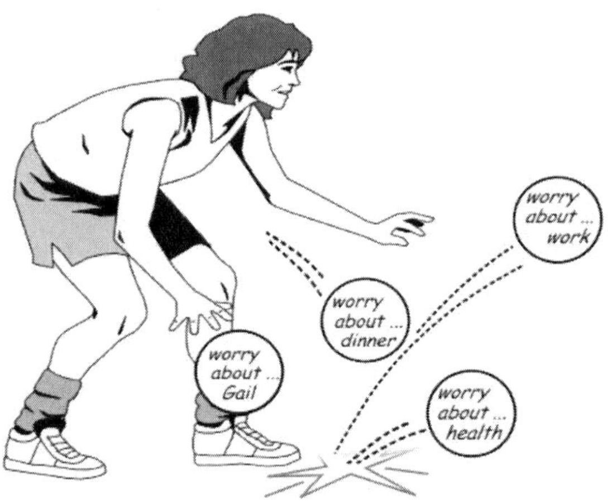

I know I'm not the only one that thinks (or used to think) like this. The belief that we have to worry about one thing or another is misguided. Why would we ever have to worry? This is another thing the mind lies to us about. It tells us that worrying will keep us or our loved ones safe. Did you feel safe the last time you worried? Not me. Not even a little bit. Worrying creates the feeling of fear. In this scenario, when we stop engaging in the act of worrying, the feeling of worry or fear will simply dissolve.

Do you think that worrying will give you control? My mother was full of fear, at least during the period of her life when I knew her. She not only worried about me when I was in her womb, she worried about me whenever I left the house, with or without her. One time, we were driving through a somewhat rough neighborhood in Brooklyn, and I must have said something about someone walking down the street. I don't recall what I said, but I do remember my mother's response. My mother said, "Don't look at him. You never know who's going to pull out a gun and shoot you."

Really? What was I supposed to do with a comment like that? Never look at anyone for the rest of my life? Well, maybe, if my mother had her way. I know my mother was scared. I know she wanted me to be safe, but her worrying became a way for her to try to control my behavior.

In my own case, when Gail was driving to or from Albuquerque without me, I probably said to Gail more than once, "Why didn't you call? I was worried." That was my own attempt to control his behavior.

Most of us have had the experience of feeling that someone is trying to control us with their worrying, even if we haven't identified it as such. I had one client who was so tied to his mother's worrying that at the age of fifty-two he was still calling or visiting every single day so she wouldn't worry.

Next time you find yourself worrying about someone, just check to see if you want them to behave in a certain way to take care of you. Besides the fact that trying to control or manage someone else's life is wrong in many ways, it's not an effective strategy. Think about how you feel when you want someone to do something and they don't do it. Most people get agitated and upset. This is not an emotional state that you actively seek. Instead of having control, you probably feel out of control and at their mercy. *If he would just call, I would be okay. If she would just turn out the lights, I wouldn't have to worry.* When we do this, we put the locus of control for our state of mind outside of ourselves. And it never works. We end up feeling more out of control. Instead of waiting for someone else to do or say something to take care of you or your feelings, ask yourself what you need and find a way to meet this need for yourself.

And when dealing with others, there is a difference between the courtesy of letting someone know you will be late so they can plan accordingly and buying into their worrying and feeling controlled by it. You can take responsibility for living in integrity without feeling obligated to take care of someone else's feelings.

Do you think worrying will create connection? Sometimes we use worry as a way to feel close to someone and keep them on our minds. A woman at one of my workshops said that she was worried about her son who was currently overseas in a combat zone. She believed it was her job to worry, and to help with the task, she watched the news every day and had trouble sleeping and focusing. She seemed to believe that worrying would help keep him safe and also seemed to feel that it would be wrong not to worry.

But there was another element at play. The worrying served to keep him in her awareness and give her the feeling of being connected. And yes, when you worry about someone, they are on your mind constantly, and it might even feel that they are in the same room with you. But you can have this same result by recalling your favorite times with them or imagining them safe and warm in their beds.

If you are going to use your imagination, shouldn't it be in your favor? When you think about it, worrying is simply using your imagination to make yourself crazy. With a simple shift in awareness, you can continue doing what you are doing (employing your imagination) to create a joyful experience.

Deal with the next feeling that arises.

During one of my presentations, a man in the audience shared that he could let go of the worry, but then he felt guilty. This goes back to the belief that we are supposed to worry, that somehow our feeling bad and agitated is what someone else wants or expects from us, or that something bad is going to happen if we let go of our vigilance. It also suggests that if we stop worrying, it means we don't care.

Hopefully, you are recognizing how absurd some of our thinking is. Nonetheless, we now have a new feeling to deal with: guilt. Similar to worry, we take the noun "guilt" and turn it into a verb by doing guilt or feeling guilty. But it is interesting to contemplate what guilt actually is. Beyond the legal sense of being proclaimed guilty for some violation of the law, we usually use the word "guilt" to describe a feeling we have after doing something we deem wrong or imagine to be wrong. In other words, we sometimes have a sense of guilt over an imagined offense. This is the kind of guilt my clients often report experiencing. They feel guilty about something they imagine has happened because of something they did or didn't do, with no verification from the outside world.

Client: "I'm afraid my friend is mad at me because I didn't go to the concert with her last month."

Me: "Well, have you asked her?"

Client: "No, I'm afraid to call in case she's mad."

Me: "What if she's not?"

Client: "Oh, is that a possibility?"

The other issue here, besides feeling guilty for something you don't even know has happened, is taking responsibility for someone else's feelings. Sometimes people are going to be unhappy with your choices. What they do with their feelings is their responsibility, not yours. And in case you missed it, I'll say it again: We are not in charge of other people's feelings. Most of us don't know how to manage our own feelings, so how could we possibly know how someone else wants their feelings handled? Talk about a setup!

Our imagined offenses can include things that we are secretly glad we did, like miss our twentieth high school reunion because there's no one there we want to talk to anyway. But we worry that others will think badly of us, and then we take on the feeling of guilt. In these situations, it's helpful to notice that we would do exactly the same thing the next time, and there might even be an accompanying feeling of pride about it under the guilt.

In *The Sedona Method* chart of emotions, guilt falls into the category of grief. Initially, this might not make sense to us. We think of grief as feeling loss over someone or something. But grief also encompasses feeling that you overlooked something, that you didn't do something you could or should have done. When you feel you might have missed something (that could have prevented an outcome), you may turn to guilt. This is where grief intersects with guilt and the belief that worrying is helpful. The mind tells you things would have turned out differently if you had spent more time worrying. Then you wouldn't be feeling guilty now.

And you can deal with it in the same way you can deal with any other feeling: be with it, notice the accompanying sensations in the body, let those sensations move as they do, and notice that they are not attached to you.

Other feelings that may arise when you stop worrying include anger and sadness. Sometimes it feels easier to tell someone you are worried than to tell them that you are angry or disappointed. If you remember that worry is a strategy to avoid feelings, this won't be a surprise. You can go back to what you have learned about being with anger or sadness and allow it to move and release. Then take appropriate action when necessary. And that may involve doing or saying something that makes you uncomfortable. You will live through it.

Okay, on to the next habit that had previously stopped me from writing this book and doing so many other things.

Procrastination

By definition, procrastination is postponing doing something. We put off doing things we dislike, but even more than that, we put off doing things that will bring up feelings we don't like. Firing an employee, starting a diet, and saying no to a friend are some of the things we may try to avoid by postponing.

The habit of procrastinating is simply another strategy to avoid what we may be feeling. Procrastination can also be a reactive response to someone, including yourself, telling you what to do. When you tell yourself that you have to do anything, there's another part of you that immediately chimes in with something like, "You can't make me." Becoming aware of this internal dialogue will dissipate some of its power over you.

One tool to avoid this reactive response is to become curious, to wonder when it will happen. When you wonder when it will happen, you are recognizing that, sooner or later, it will get done. When you shift the internal conversation from "it must be done" to acknowledgment and curiosity, you free up the energy that resistance pulls from you. I've used this strategy to clear my desk area, my clothes closet, and the garage—all things I could have procrastinated about for long periods of time.

30-Second Play Break

Think about a project you've been putting off. Instead of telling yourself "I have to get it done" say to yourself "I wonder when I'm going to get to that" and notice what happens.

As with all feelings and habits, resistance to procrastination gives it more energy and keeps it active for even longer than it would be on its own. When we tell ourselves it is not okay to put off making that phone call, walking the dog, or writing the book, we end up putting it off even longer. Instead, we can give ourselves permission to enjoy being lazy for an hour, a day, or a week. Of course, this is impacted by whatever else is going on in our lives. If we've been pushing hard for years, it may take a week or even a month until we're ready to start that next project.

Intentional procrastination can sometimes be a good thing, and making the procrastination conscious will inform you as to whether or not that is so.

Lusting

Once again, with lusting, we have taken the feeling of lust or want and turned it into a habit or even an obsession. We daydream about the perfect partner, the dream job, and the oodles of money in the bank. The crazy thing is that we think this might actually help us get what we want. As mentioned in Chapter 2, many goal workshops teach that we have to lust if we really want whatever our goal is.

But if you think about something you really want—whether it's money, peace, or a relationship—you can feel in your body that sense of not having or not being enough. When you want or lust for something, you are very literally reminding yourself of lack or limitation. Similar to worrying, lusting creates a feeling of lack, and when that is what you are paying attention to, that is what ends up multiplying.

Has anyone ever told you that you must not really want whatever you have stated you want or that you have to really, really want it before you can have it? It might have made you pretty angry. My guess is that there are some things you want (and have been wanting for a long time) really badly, and you still don't have them. If wanting is what it takes, don't you think you would have it by now?

The truth is that wanting affirms a feeling of lack in the body. Each time you say you want or need something, you will notice that it creates a longing, a feeling of not having. This then becomes the mantra we put out to the world: "I want it and I don't have it; I want it and I can't have it."

Lester Levenson, who developed The Sedona Method™, coined the term "hootlessness," defined as being in a state of not giving a hoot, of being happy with it, happy without it. Lester said, "Even the most impossible becomes completely possible when you are fully released on it, and you know that you are fully released when you don't give a hoot." [6]

It's part of the human experience to want things, but the more we can let go of any feelings that we must have something, or that it will not be okay if we don't have something, the more ease we feel in our lives. When we are at ease, things seem to happen effortlessly and we are more apt to take action. The woman who has been trying to get pregnant for many years and finally decides to adopt, then finds herself pregnant six months later, has probably entered into a state of hootlessness.

As you learn to notice the feelings triggered each time you go into wanting and allow them to let go, you can return to a sense of well-being. In this place of well-being, it is much easier to allow life to unfold as it does and gratefully accept the riches that come to you each day.

During my experience in the Santa Fe jewelry store mentioned earlier, the good mood I had been in was immediately gone when I began to want all the earrings. Even while still in the store, I had enough awareness of the shift to ask myself what had just happened. This doesn't always occur to me in the moment, but I'm grateful when it does because it can prevent hours of bad mood. As I stayed with myself, I was able to recognize that I was experiencing the feeling of lust directed at the jewelry. I simply asked myself if I could just feel the sensations and let them move through and dissolve. It just took a couple of breaths and I felt better.

This is an example of a time when I was able to catch the feeling before it turned into a habit. Sometimes we can do this; other times lusting is more of a background noise, like someone nagging at us from the next room. If you stop and pay attention to the background, you may find beliefs and feelings associated with making big changes in your life, changes that may scare the heck out of you. If you are willing to dig in and confront the fear, you may find the answer to what you have been missing.

Or, you could just eat something.

Overindulging

Just thinking about writing on the topic of overindulging creates a longing to walk away from my writing and get a snack. My conscious mind knows this is a destructive habit and my body knows this is a destructive habit, so what gives? This is definitely one of those programs that appears to run on automatic. When we're not paying attention, addiction seems to take over.

A mentor of mine once said, "I got caught in addiction." What a lovely and gentle way of phrasing this experience. Similar to a tidal wave, addiction scoops us up and spits us out. Overindulging is not always tied to addiction. We will occasionally make conscious choices to drink or eat too much (as at a wedding), or even watch too much television. It's the times when the overindulging becomes unconscious or driven that we are using it as an addictive strategy. These two words, "addictive" and "strategy," used together may seem strange, but addiction is a strategy to cope with or avoid feelings, like any other habit.

To free yourself from addiction, it helps to understand what you get from it. For instance, beyond the natural nurturing qualities of food, we sometimes think that food is love, especially if we were raised by someone who expressed love by feeding us. If one or both of our parents were drinkers, we may (subconsciously) believe that drinking will create a bond with them. Or we may think we are in control when we work out obsessively.

When you can identify the feeling you get from the addiction or overindulgence, it allows you to look for more constructive ways to address the need. Awareness occurs when you step back from the activities of your mind and emotions to observe. It can help you identify what the feeling is and also make you more conscious when you are engaging in automatic behaviors.

In *The Observing Self*, author Arthur Deikman talks about the self-witness and defines the observing self as the transparent center, that which is aware.[7] He compares awareness to the surface of a pond, where thoughts, feelings, and other mental activities occur as splashes and ripples in the water. When we cultivate awareness around our activities, it creates a momentary pause during which we can choose our actions.

A gentle first step towards awareness would be to invite yourself to simply notice what is happening. For example, if you know you'd like to change your habit of grabbing a cookie each time you pass the kitchen, you can tell yourself to just watch this happening. The first few times, you may find that you catch yourself just as you've finished the cookie or as you're eating it. But eventually, you'll start catching yourself sooner and will catch yourself right before you grab the cookie. Then you will be able to make a choice about whether or not to eat it. If you've seen the movie, *Groundhog Day*, you may be reminded of the puddle that Bill Murray falls into day after day, until one day, he catches himself and steps around it.

Criticizing Self and Others

As with some of the other habits we've covered, when we engage in criticizing, we have taken something neutral and turned it into something to use against ourselves or others. There's really nothing wrong with some constructive criticism, and when it's well delivered, we can grow and change because of it. Receiving feedback from the outside world can be incredibly helpful, and knowing how to assess and evaluate our own work and behavior is part of the learning process. But how often do you follow the rules for giving constructive feedback when you're talking to yourself? Probably not too often. It's much more time efficient to skip over the positive assessment of all the stuff you're doing well and go straight for the jugular. The same thing applies when you are judging or criticizing others in your mind. We often save the niceties for when we are actually *voicing* our opinions to others. And then we behave (maybe) as the polite adults we were taught to be when giving our input.

Rules of the Game

What are some of the rules for giving others feedback that we could apply to ourselves?

1. Show respect.

This rule is by far the most overlooked and crucial when we evaluate our own progress. Being respectful would include a careful assessment of the situation. In the book scenario, when I was initially writing, it was important to take into account the deal I made with myself to just keep writing, get the first draft written, and go back later to add references and delete repetition. Keeping these facts in mind, when I reviewed my writing midstream I was able to give myself credit for what was accomplished, rather than criticize what was missing.

2. Explain why it's a problem.

This rule is a continuation of respect. I explained to myself, sometimes as I would to a child, that I would be out of integrity with myself and unhappy if I didn't finish the book or write it to meet my expectations. This helped me find the internal motivation to keep going. Reminding myself that the book was important to me helped me stay in integrity with myself, and it was a better motivator than self-scolding.

3. Be accommodating.

This is an interesting rule when applied to oneself. It involves asking the person receiving the feedback how she would like to receive it. Would she prefer e-mail or a private face-to-face conversation?

What would it feel like if you told the voice that you would like to receive that feedback in writing instead of going through the day with a voice that says, "Not good enough," or some variation thereof? Though it sounds cumbersome, it could be considerably more productive.

4. Determine your goals.

When we give feedback to an employee, we do it with a specific outcome in mind. We have a complaint, but also a preferred outcome. Often, we overlook this in self-criticism. There is no suggestion of another outcome, just complaints about the way it's being done, or not being done. When we can give ourselves this important piece of information, then a plan can be made to make that happen. Without it, we may feel like we have a boss we will never be able to please.

5. Be specific.

Feedback can spiral out of control when everything is on the table and incidents that were resolved long ago are dredged up. I see this happen in couples counseling on a pretty regular basis. Just recently, someone was complaining about her partner invalidating her feelings, an issue that had been resolved several months earlier. Not only is this strategy unproductive, it also keeps us stuck in the past and keeps the old issues alive. If we stick to the specifics and the current behavior that's not working, it is much easier to focus on the outcome we want.

6. Leave it alone.

Once you've expressed your complaint, leave it alone. We all hate being nagged, and when we do it to ourselves, it's even more invasive. When offering criticism to yourself, don't rehash your complaints over and over. When you continue to offer the same feedback, there's an underlying belief that you won't do whatever it is you're complaining to yourself about. Instead of undermining yourself, try trusting that you will follow through.

That Was Then, This Is Now

Setting: In the middle of a therapy session with a client.
Characters: Me as Critic; Me as Melanie
The old feedback conversation:
(Critic) Melanie, I can't believe you haven't written in a week.
(Melanie) Hush. I can't think about this now.
(Critic) Well, when are you going to think about it, next year?
(Melanie) Hush. I'm with a client.
(Critic) You're always with clients. When are you going to make the book a priority?
(Melanie) Hush!

We can see in this short example how I've broken all the rules. As my own critic, I was disrespectful of myself (and my client), I said nothing about why it was a problem, I was definitely not accommodating, I did not offer any solutions or goals, and I was not apt to leave it alone.

Setting: In my sitting area where I journal and meditate.
Characters: Me as Critic; Me as Coach; Me as Melanie
The new feedback conversation:
(Critic) Melanie, you haven't written in a week. When can we discuss this?
(Melanie) You're right. This is important, but I have to get some things done. Can we talk later?
(Critic now sounding more like a coach) Yes. What time would work?
(Melanie) 11:00 a.m.

At 11:00 a.m.
(Coach) Melanie, I know you've been very busy, but I'm concerned that you won't reach your goal of having the book finished by the end of the month if you keep getting distracted.
(Melanie) Yes, you're right. I don't know what to do.
(Coach) Well, how about writing for fifteen minutes two times a day?
(Melanie) Only fifteen minutes? That feels doable.
(Coach) Great. That's the plan. Fifteen minute two times a day for a week. And then I'll check back with you same time next week.

Whew, that feels better. And now I have something I can work with.

Taking Action

A great way to eliminate the impact of two bad habits is to do them simultaneously. Add procrastination to some other bad habit. Decide to intentionally procrastinate when it comes to worrying, overindulging, criticizing, and lusting. "Oh, I'll get up in an hour to get that cookie." "I don't have time now to worry. I'll do it tomorrow." "I'm too busy to figure out all the things I did wrong. I'll put it on the to-do list." In fact, you can give yourself permission to procrastinate these things forever! You never have to get to them. Leave them on the list for as long as you want and give yourself some approval for doing such a good job of procrastinating!

Speaking of to-do lists, if you have recognized some new and old habits in reading this chapter, now is a great time to take an inventory of your habits.

Play Break

Find some colored pens or pencils and make a list of all the habits you would like to be free of.

In doing this inventory, list all the habits you know don't serve you. Then do an honest inquiry. Ask yourself, "Which of these habits am I willing to do something about?" or, "Which is most important to address first?" Then, using my suggestions and adding any of your own, create a plan for letting go of or transforming those habits. Be sure to acknowledge your progress, big or small. What we pay attention to multiplies.

4

Dealing with Others

We have now navigated through our own blocking thoughts, feelings, habits, and behaviors that interfere with living a stress free life. Do we really have to deal with what other people think, feel, do, and say? Well, unless you want to live your life as a hermit (which I realize might have some appeal), you are likely to encounter some input from the people in your life—even though it's none of their business.

"What?" you say.

I said your life is not their business. It may be easy for you to recognize this when it comes to strangers or casual acquaintances. With family, it may be more difficult. Others behave as if they have the right to know what you are doing with your body and your time and what thoughts you are thinking and what you may be feeling. More than likely, you also believe you have the right to know these things about close friends and family. You don't. The sharing of one's life with another is a gift, one you can choose to offer. And if offered by another, you can choose to accept or reject it.

Many aspects of your life may be affected by significant others. It may feel important to know what they are thinking and feeling. It still doesn't make it your right to know. If you are in relationship with someone who withholds crucial information (from your perspective), you can choose whether or not to stay in that relationship, even with a family member.

We already know how challenging it is for each of us to manage our own experience (including our own thoughts, feelings, and habits). How can anyone possibly be designed to handle someone else's? It would be overwhelming. Even raising a child, whom we are supposed to have some management over, has its limits. As parents, it is our job to teach them well.

Children are entitled to their thoughts and feelings. Each child comes into the world with a unique blueprint. A parent's job is to nurture and allow the beauty of that child to shine. And to allow the child to have his or her feelings.

We are each on our own journey. Our choices, including our mistakes, belong to us. This is not to say we do not ask for help or guidance when needed and offer it when asked. But it's important to remember that as much as we may think we know how someone else should lead their life, we never have the entire story. And even if we did, it still wouldn't be our job to tell them. It's not our job to tell them how to live, and it's not their job to tell us how to live.

Despite the fact that it's not anybody else's job to tell us what they think or feel about what we are doing, it's inevitably going to happen. The good news is that dealing with input from others is actually easier than dealing with internal chatter. At least we can walk away from others.

What Others May Be Thinking

How much time do we spend wondering and worrying about what someone else may think about us? From what I can tell, way too much. There's a book with a great title, and I quote that title to my clients regularly: *What You Think of Me is None of My Business*, by Terry Cole-Whittaker. A similar quote, "Your opinion of me is none of my business," is attributed to several different authors. Whoever said it first doesn't really matter. It's true. Approximately 99 percent (okay, I made that statistic up, but I'm sure it's close to accurate) of what someone else thinks of you says more about them and their past than it says about you.

Everybody's perception, including yours, is colored by personal life experience. We see the world and others through our own filters. Our opinions of others are determined by what we believe is okay for us—and therefore, the world in general. If you were raised by conservative parents, pole dancing may be repulsive to you. If you were raised by liberal parents, pole dancing may be the greatest thing to come along in years. Why would the person who is engaging in pole dancing want to be influenced by your parents? She's still dealing with the expectations of her own parents, whether they are dead or alive. And the same is true for all of us. I have my own internal parental recordings that replay regularly. Why would I want to be influenced or controlled by what others think of me?

This is not to say that I won't want input from time to time to help me make a decision. There are people in my life I trust and respect, and if there is wisdom to be shared, I want it. But I have learned to be wary of all those offering unsolicited advice. "No thanks," I say to that!

So what do you do when you are offered opinions you don't want? The same thing you do when your own mind starts to chatter. As soon as you become aware of agitation, (which could feel like wanting to get out of there, feeling bad about yourself, or a sense of defensiveness), stop, take a breath, and notice what's happening. The moment you take to breathe is an opportunity to catch yourself before reacting.

Reaction and Response

In our daily interactions, when we feel fully present and engaged, we respond based on current circumstances. At other times, when we may not be quite as present, we get easily triggered and reactive.

We become reactive when the present moment gets associated with an unpleasant experience from the past. The reaction happens so quickly that we don't recognize what's happening. Rebecca, a client who came in for couples counseling with her husband, demonstrated reactive behavior beautifully. In one of our early sessions together, Rebecca's husband suggested that she take some time off. Rebecca immediately flew into a rage and started explaining and defending her need to work eighty hours a week. When we dug under the reaction, Rebecca shared that she felt she was being attacked, and under that, she had feelings of not doing a good enough job as wife and mother. Her husband's comment reminded her of how her father had told her what she wasn't doing right about many things in her life. She was unable to see that her husband's comment came out of concern for her well-being.

Rebecca's insecurities about herself (arising from previous relationships) fueled her reaction to her husband. By staying present to the reaction, she was able to see that what she really needed from her husband was recognition about how hard she was trying. The part of Rebecca that held the wound from the past longed for reassurance. We can see from this how juicy and informative our reactions can be if we explore where they are coming from instead of blaming others for them.

When our reactions go unchecked, they take an entirely different path. Reactions create fixed thought patterns and positions. They limit your ability to be in the present moment because they represent a solidified response. Reactions create rigidities in your belief system and in your body. When you react, there is no room to experience the current moment. Our reactions are no different than the knee jerk response we get when the doctor hits a certain nerve with his little hammer. The body has no choice. The nerve has been struck and the muscle automatically responds.

These emotional and mental reactions or habits can prevent us from deepening our experience. We don't respond authentically in the moment but with a preconceived notion of what is intended and what the outcome will be. Because reactions are rigid, there is usually no room to take in any new information and modify our position. Reactions have a big investment in being right. Christine Caldwell, one of my teachers at Naropa University, says that being right is one of the most addictive habits around. Many years ago, I found myself in a double bind. No matter which approach I took, I was going to be told I was wrong. In a moment of brilliance, I thought to myself, *Oh, there's a lesson here. I don't get to be right.* It was a major transition point in my life. I can see now that being right (or wrong) is a feature of reaction, and I can go below that reaction to see what I might really be feeling.

When dealing with others, I recommend this as your first action step: notice the experience it brings up in you. Is it a reaction or a response? A great way to determine this really fast (in less than thirty seconds) is to notice what is happening in your body. A reaction will cause some type of tightness or rigidity in the body. It may be felt in the stomach, the chest, the arms, the jaw—almost anywhere. I can feel a reaction as a knot in my stomach, a tingling in my arms, or a catch in my throat. A response based in the current moment will solicit a more relaxed, open feeling in the body. I spent the entire first year of my training in body-oriented psychotherapy learning to distinguish between these two in my body. So if it takes a while to become proficient at this, be patient with yourself.

If you recognize that you are feeling reactive towards another, you may want to take some time with yourself before saying or doing anything. Let's say that the other person's comment reminds you of something your dad used to say frequently that you didn't like. If the person you're interacting with is someone you know well, you can be direct and say, "That reminds me of how my dad used to react, and I feel blamed when you say those things."

If it is your boss or someone you don't know well, you might not want to go that route. Instead, it can be helpful to find an internal response before saying something out loud to the other person. Here are a couple options to play with internally: *Huh, isn't it interesting that he thinks that?* or *Wow. Isn't it interesting that she thinks I care what she says?*

This internal conversation will take less than thirty seconds, and will help you get centered in yourself and recognize that you don't have to be influenced by another's opinion. Then you can calmly respond with whatever is appropriate under the circumstances. When the situation is full of emotion, you may need several breaths and several internal conversations. And your best response might be to stay silent. Remember, you can always walk away and come back later with a response. The internal dialogue becomes even more important in this circumstance. Recognizing that there is an internal dialogue will help you shift the locus of control for your state of mind from other to self.

When a friend or family member offers an opinion you haven't asked for and don't want, you might be willing to be more open with them. You can tell them "thanks, but no thanks." Say this in the kindest way you can. If they don't get it the first time, repeat it until they do.

Worried that they will be offended? Well, that takes us right into dealing with the feelings of others.

Dealing with the Feelings of Others

Other people's feelings are not your job, not your responsibility! Yes, you want to be kind and courteous if you can, but their feelings belong to them and they get to deal with them. This doesn't mean you get to do or say whatever you feel like to whomever you feel like. That's just rude. But when you tell the truth about what you are experiencing or feeling in a direct, honest, and kind way, ultimately, that is all you are responsible for.

You cannot manage the response or reaction you will get from others when you speak what is true for you. And when the other person reacts, you may then have to go through the whole cycle again, dealing with your own feelings that result from their reaction or response. This part of the cycle, dealing with your own thoughts and feelings, is your job, your responsibility. Think of it as a rather sophisticated dance, one in which you each have your own designated dance space. You get to dance with your feelings; they get to dance with theirs. It is as simple as that.

So without being callous, how do you respond when others around you are hurt or offended? Well, first I suggest softening your heart. I know, nobody's ever taught you how to soften your heart. But it's not that hard. When you recognize that the thoughts and feelings of another are not about you (and remember, they almost never are), you can see the person in front of you as someone who is simply scared or hurting.

When you see others in this way, it's easier to feel compassion for what they may be experiencing. When you feel compassion, you can act from compassion. You might simply respond by being present or you might say, "I hear that you are angry (or sad, or upset)." Sometimes a simple validation can go a long way. There is an intervention in the field of psychotherapy called reflecting. Basically, you repeat back what the client has just said to you. When I first learned of this intervention, I had an aversion to it, believing it to be patronizing. Interestingly enough, I didn't have a problem using it in movement (mirroring or repeating back someone's movement so they could see it outside of themselves), so for the first year or so in private practice, I only used the reflecting intervention in movement.

And then it happened. A client came in and told me a somewhat complicated and convoluted story about her memories of her mother. As she told me the story, she referenced her back and her stomach. Because I was confused, I repeated back what I had heard. "So you're feeling pulled from behind and pushed from the front."

My client's eyes got very wide and she said, "Wow, I never looked at it like that before."

She then got in touch with how much she felt both held back and pushed by her mother. She thought I was a genius.

And I had a newfound respect for reflection. Sometimes, people just need to be heard. You can say, "I get that you're angry," or "I'm sorry you're so upset." If you can genuinely feel this, they will feel it from you and it just may have an impact on them.

Wanting to manage or control other people's behaviors is as natural as breathing. We all have ideas about how other people should act, especially in our presence.

My dear friend and dance teacher, Jessica, tells a great story about this. Some years ago, her home was broken into, and while she was on the phone with police dispatch, her twelve-year-old son was yelling and throwing things.

The dispatch officer said to Jessica, "Ma'am, could you please get him to calm down?"

Now, if the officer had known Jessica, she wouldn't have asked such a silly question. I can see the scene in my mind's eye now. Mama bear, Jessica, was unworried about the officer's discomfort. She knew that her son was entitled to feel and express his feelings. Instead of complying with the request, she simply said, "No, I will not."

End of conversation. Deal with it.

Side note: As a result of allowing his rage, by the time the police showed up at their home, he was fine. Jessica, on the other hand, admits to going into a freeze state and not feeling her own feelings. While two weeks later she was still processing what had happened, her son was long done with it.

Other people's behaviors (which could include expressing a feeling) can often be uncomfortable for us. Those behaviors may be healthy (as in the above scenario) or unhealthy (as in overdrinking or overeating). We often try to manage our discomfort by controlling the behaviors of others, believing that if they would just calm down or stop drinking, we wouldn't have to feel uncomfortable. It's really just another attempt to avoid dealing with our own feelings. We reason that if we can control what's going on outside of us, we won't have to deal with the feelings that are arising inside us. But we can't. Well, maybe once in a while or in some partial degree, but the strategy is not an effective one in the long run.

If you are constantly trying to manage or control what is happening in the outside world (which includes everything and everyone that is not you), you will run out of energy and will feel at the mercy of the behavior of others. Every single time you try to control anything or anyone outside yourself, you feel controlled by it.

Recently, I was having a conversation with a coaching client about money. He really wanted to control money. I'm pretty sure he's not alone in that. "Dennis," I said, "it's impossible to want to control money and not feel controlled by money."

He argued, "But if I could control money, I wouldn't feel controlled by it.

I replied, "But you're not *controlling* money, you are *trying* to control money. It's different."

"But I want to control money," he admitted.

"I know," I said. "But there's no way to want to control money without being at its mercy."

"Damn," he replied.

30-Second Play Break

Stop and think about something or someone you are wanting to control. Maybe you'd like it to stop raining. Perhaps you want your spouse to stop drinking. Or maybe you want a patient to be more compliant. Let yourself feel what wanting to control a situation or another person's actions feels like in your body. Then, just for now, try letting go of wanting to control it.

Tips for Successful Relating

1. Know what is and is not your business. Stay out of that which is not your business.

This first tip is, to some extent, a reiteration of what we have already covered in this chapter. This tip is the most important—and most violated—component to healthy relationships, and it deserves further exploration and emphasis.

So often, we take responsibility for another person's well-being (or what our idea of that is), and we try to get them to do what we think is best for them or us. The problem with this is that most of the time, nobody asked for our opinions or help. When we offer our help, advice, and opinions, we feel and believe that we are being generous, and we expect people will be grateful that we want to help. But when that help is unsolicited and unwanted, the person we are offering to help may not feel grateful. Instead, they may feel resistant and resentful. This can leave us feeling unappreciated and resentful. What a mess!

In the 1980s, A. Justin Sterling, founder of the Sterling Institute of Relationship, used to say in his women's workshops, "It's not your job to manage his life. That's a $50,000 a year job. If he's not paying you $50,000 a year to run his life, stay out of it." (With inflation, it's more like five times that now.) This has been a great tip for me in my marriage. Yes, there are many times I have to catch myself, and I sometimes fail. But as a general rule, my husband's business is not automatically my business just because we're married.

My dear friend Judy Borich, author of *Touch and Go, The Nature of Intimacy*, tells a story about this issue. In her therapy practice, she was working with an older couple who had been married for forty years. They came in to see her about an issue they were having with their daughter. During the session, Judy asked them what their secret was for their obviously happy and successful marriage. Their response was, "We mind our manners."

All too often, when we have a close or intimate relationship with someone, we think we don't have to mind our manners. "Oh, it's just Jenny. She knows me; she'll get over it." I don't think we realize how often we are being disrespectful to our loved ones.

Next time you feel like putting in your two cents, remember to stay out of what's not your business and mind your manners.

If you believe you're just trying to be helpful, doing some self-exploration on what is driving that can be enlightening. What you think is sincere altruism may be motivated by desires that could surprise you, such as wanting approval or connection. If you take the time to become aware of your motivation, you can simply let it go and focus your energy in a more productive direction.

2. Keep your agreements.

Keeping your word is probably the single most important thing you can do to establish trust in a relationship.

I don't mind if someone tells me they aren't going to do something. But if they tell me they are going to do something and they don't, that upsets me. Often, we are afraid to turn down a request, so we'll say yes just to make someone happy or keep the peace. We may really believe that we're going to do whatever we have committed to and then find ourselves procrastinating about it. Then we avoid the person or the subject and start to feel bad about ourselves. And then the relationship has another dent.

Most of us are also guilty of saying we'll "try" when we're pretty sure it's not going to happen. We are trying to hedge our bets. Lester Levenson has been quoted as saying that trying is wanting approval for something you have no intention of doing. When someone tells me they will try to make it to an event I've invited them to, I count that as a no.

If you know that you're not going to do something, say so. If you fully intend to and something changes, say so as soon as you know. Most people are open to renegotiating agreements if you keep them apprised of what's happening.

3. Have fun together.

In *Fighting for Your Marriage* by Howard J. Markman, play is said to be the single best indicator of a relationship's long-term success.[8] The fun we have with others keeps us connected and gives us the juice to get through the challenging times.

Most of the couples who come in to see me for counseling admit that it's been a long time since they've had any fun together. One of the first assignments I give them is to find something they can enjoy doing as a couple.

This doesn't only apply to intimate relationships. Back in my twenties, when I was going on my first job interviews, I knew I'd have a much better chance at getting the job offer if I could get the interviewer to laugh. When I interviewed with Frank, a very serious and intense guy, it took me a while, but I knew I had the job when he finally chuckled at something I said. The interview also set the tone for our relationship for the year we worked together. Others in our department were intimidated by him, but our relationship was (relatively) fun and easy.

If you work in an environment with people who never laugh, the day is going to feel very long. You may initially feel silly and need to muster courage, but find something to lighten the mood. You'll find it easier to get the job done well.

4. Feel your feelings.

We have already covered this as it related to your relationship with yourself, but experiencing your feelings is also important for healthy relationships with others. When we aren't in touch with our own feelings, it's very easy to find fault with others.

When I was still living in New York, I had a housemate who was a great guy and a great friend. He was meticulous, quiet when needed, available when asked, and overall, a wonderful person to have around. But I started to feel annoyed with him at every turn. If he was sleeping when I awoke, I was bothered that I had to be quiet. If he was awake, I felt resentful that I had to talk to him. After a couple of weeks feeling this way, I recognized that it wasn't about him. I just wanted my space and needed to say so. We managed to maintain a close friendship even after he moved out.

Christine Caldwell, my teacher and mentor at Naropa University mentioned earlier, taught about the illness cycle. This is a concept she developed to explain what happens when we don't feel our feelings. The cycle consists of four phases: desensitization, projection, rejection, and desynchronization. In the first phase, we cut off from the current experience and ignore the sensations in our body. Because emotions are felt in the body, we must shut them off at the level of sensation to effectively avoid our feelings.

When we push those feelings away, they often land on those we are closest to, physically or emotionally. We project the feelings we refuse to feel onto others. We may say, "She's so angry all the time," when really we feel angry.

Next we push away and reject the person we have projected the unwanted feelings onto, typically with an attitude like, *I hate being around her. She's so angry all the time.*

Finally, we move into desynchronization, where we are literally out of sync with the world and don't always understand what is happening around us, especially when it comes to emotions.

It may feel easier to blame someone else for what's going on inside you, but unfortunately, it's not very effective. Until you allow yourself to feel and then resolve the real source of your feelings, they will continue to cause disturbance.

Whenever you are angry or upset, check and see what's getting triggered or if there is something inside you that you are avoiding or judging.

5. Express gratitude.

Gratitude, like any other emotion, needs to be expressed. Let your loved ones know you're grateful for their love and equally grateful to be able to give them yours. Let your employees know you're thankful they are working with you. And let your children know you're grateful they were born to you.

Gratitude is said to be one of the most powerful healing emotions. It's one of the reasons so many spiritual teachers recommend using a gratitude journal and counting your blessings. Another good reason to focus on what you are grateful for is the principle that what you pay attention to multiplies. When you tell your partner how grateful you are for the back rubs he gives you without your having to beg for them or the chocolates he brought home yesterday, you are increasing the probability of that behavior being continued or repeated.

6. Be willing to both give and receive.

Many of the couples I work with are out of balance in their relationship with giving and receiving. We have been taught that it is better to give than receive, but the formula is incomplete. If everyone is always giving, who is available to receive what we give?

Imagine spending hours or days planning the perfect gift for a loved one. You're so excited to give it to him and enjoy his reaction. He opens the gift and says, "Great! Thanks," sets your gift down, and then says, "Now open mine." He isn't interested in receiving, just giving. He has denied you the joy of giving by withholding his own feeling of enjoyment in receiving.

All givers need recipients. We must have as many receivers as givers for the system to work on either an interpersonal or a global level. This is also true on an intrapersonal (within ourselves) level. If you are only able to experience one side of this flow, you get out of balance. If you only outflow, you eventually drain yourself and have nothing left to give. By that time, people have become used to you being the giver and never receiving. When that happens, you may become resentful of others and feel taken for granted. Yet you are the one who trained your loved ones to believe you have no needs and no capacity for receiving.

If you've reached this point or are near to it, you can take a gentle step towards receiving by asking others for little things. You can have a family member bring you a glass of ice water or ask a friend to go on a hike with you (without offering to bring the snacks). Receive a compliment with a simple, "Thank you, I really appreciate that you noticed," and resist the impulse to compliment them in return.

Cultivating the ability to both give unconditionally and receive openly is critical for healthy relationships. That does not mean we enter into the barter relationship: I'll give you this if you give me that. Giving in order to receive is a contract and has nothing to do with feeling the love that is available in both giving and receiving.

If you lean more in the direction of receiving than giving, it's time to see what you're missing by not giving to others. Again, practice in small ways: offer to bring someone a cup of tea, pay a compliment, or surprise someone with flowers.

It's also possible that you are the giver with some people and the receiver with others. Though you may be in balance when you total all your giving and receiving, each individual relationship needs to find equilibrium. Even in the relationships in which you are usually the giver, you can graciously receive words of gratitude or compliments. You will find that your heart opens more to those with whom you can enjoy both giving to and receiving from.

Most of us enjoy our relationships most of the time. Most of us will also freely admit that much of our stress is a result of those relationships. We tend to think that if they just wouldn't make so many demands and would fix their annoying behaviors, our lives would be smooth and peaceful. Not really. Your life will be smooth and peaceful when you learn how to let others be. Relationships demand growth from us and for that, we can be grateful. Remembering that in any moment, we can change the dance we are doing with a different response allows us to move away from reacting from fear or anger. In thirty seconds or less, we can transform the dance into something new and potentially, wonderful.

Part II
Preventive Strategies

5

Supportive Behaviors

The suggestions in Part I of this book can help you cope with stress relief in the moment. In addition to having strategies in place you can call on at any time, it makes sense to cultivate behaviors that support well-being. When we have practices that help us stay centered, calm, and alert, we are better prepared to handle challenges as they arise. And when we know we are competent and capable of meeting life's curveballs, we don't need to plan for them by worrying and obsessing. We can think of these behaviors as our daily doses of prevention or our well-being vitamins.

Transforming habits takes a level of commitment we sometimes don't acknowledge. Many of us have developed destructive habits based on our upbringing, but knowing that these habits don't really serve us doesn't necessarily make it easy to let them go. We employed the best strategy available to us once upon a time, and partly for ease, kept using it. For example, if you knew that you would get hit every time you questioned your parents, you learned to shut up. As an adult, you may have translated this into doing everything your boss or spouse tells you to do, without question, forgetting you have other options.

One client had been in the habit of pushing herself using negative self-talk for many years. She believed she would become lazy, get fat, and be miserable if she let up on herself.

Though no one would ever mistake her for being lazy, she was overweight and miserable. Yet, the concept of being kind to herself was foreign to her, and it has taken her years to embrace and implement both the concept and the corresponding behavior. Cognitively, she was able to understand that the habit of beating herself up was increasing the behavior she was trying to eliminate. In practice, it was very difficult to do something different.

As we all know, change can be challenging. I am an advocate of the gentle approach, inching your way in. We can take one baby step at a time or imagine that we are trying on the new strategy like a new jacket to see if we like the fit and style. Sometimes we are hesitant to try new styles, but we can assess any disadvantages and benefits and then decide after trying if we want to keep the new behaviors or discard them.

Know that you can choose what changes you want for yourself.

Gentleness

About twenty years ago, I created my own set of angel cards. I took pictures of the people and things I loved and put one quality that each most represented to me on each card with the picture. Of all the wonderful qualities my husband possesses, gentleness was the one that made it on to his card. Gail has a way of being with me that allows me to be who I am, whoever that is in the moment. It took me some time to be able to do this for myself. In fact, I remember the first time I heard myself using his words, "Careful, sweetie," to myself after burning my hand. In that moment, I knew gentleness was a pretty cool thing he was teaching me.

We often judge ourselves for our perceived shortcomings. When we receive blame from ourselves or others, we usually contract in reaction. Our muscles tense to flee and withdraw or fight and defend. We shrink a little, maybe so we won't be noticed or so we become a smaller target for attacks. Even when our reaction is to fight, we are still coming from a contracted place—even when we are fleeing from, or fighting with, ourselves.

With gentleness, we create an opening, or the opposite of contraction, which is expansion. When we feel expanded, we are able to see more options for responding.

Cultivating the habit of gentleness can be challenging if you are used to being hard on yourself. Sometimes, you can take a cue from the gentle people around you. This is what I did in the example above. Simply mimicking their words or behaviors until it comes naturally can teach you this different way of being. If you don't have someone in your life you can mimic, you can think about how you treat others. Is there a child you treat with love and compassion? Could you pretend that you are speaking to that child when you speak to yourself?

If you think about it, you probably speak more harshly to yourself than to anyone else in your life. Some of us wouldn't dream of saying to others the things we say to ourselves. What if, just for a day, you refused to say anything to yourself that you wouldn't say to another? And then do that again for another day, a week, a month, forever?

30-Second Play Break

Think of one thing you say to yourself that you wouldn't say to another. Write it down. For the next twenty-four hours notice how often you say this. As best you can, do this without judging yourself. When you bring awareness to how often it happens you are taking the first step towards doing something different.

Curiosity

When I think of curiosity, the images that come to mind include exploring new neighborhoods and opening gifts, not knowing what I will find. Mystery goes hand in hand with curiosity.

This is the quality that went on my youngest stepdaughter's angel card. Emma was a precocious and daring child when it came to listening to her parents. One day when I asked her to do something, she looked back at me with eyes that said, *What are you going to do if I don't?* Interestingly, I also had a dog at the time that would respond with a similar look. When I created my angel cards, instead of interpreting this look as defiance, I went with curiosity, which I believe was the real motivator behind Emma's behavior (and that of Kina, my pretty little dog, too). The words that went on the card were, "What would happen if I tried doing this differently?"

Curiosity is a playful state that demands presence. It's very different from the analytical mind that tries to find solutions through thought. When we get curious, we don't assume we already know the answer and just have to figure it out. There's a recognition we don't know what's around the bend, literally or metaphorically.

Curiosity allows for mystery. When I can truly be curious about when the book will be finished or even if readers will find it relevant, I step out of attachment to outcome and find the expansive state I am looking for.

Curiosity demands presence. We can be curious about the future, but we cannot be curious *in* the future. We can only be curious right now.

If you've lost your connection to curiosity, all you need do is hang around a toddler or a puppy for five minutes. Watching how they explore the world can be a reminder that you once looked at everything in this way, and you can again. Alternatively, do an art project, take a walk in the woods, or try to solve a mind-bender puzzle.

To evoke a state of curiosity, go to a museum or park and look at a painting or a tree. Ask it to speak to you. I know, I know, they aren't literally going to speak to you, but you can allow yourself to imagine that they do have something to show you or tell you about yourself. If you can just be with them, and even wonder why you were drawn to that particular painting or tree, you may learn something that will surprise you.

Persistence

"Just keep writing." That's what I was telling myself when I began writing this book. "Even if you don't know where you're going, even if you're repeating yourself, even if you're writing crap, just sit down and write. Sort it out later."

Persistence is not the same thing as discipline. It calls on the stubborn part of me that knows what she wants and knows how to get it. It's rare that I get to consciously employ her. More often than not, I have to tell her, "Not now," or "Let it go." But she was very useful with this book.

Persistence is the quality I put on Harald's angel card. Harald was my lab/Australian shepherd mix who we also proclaimed was the pushiest dog ever. The saying on his card was, "I lovingly stand fast in achieving what I desire." Dogs are such great role models for persistence. They don't give up easily and they don't (usually) get nasty about it, either. They just want what they want and are going to do whatever it takes to get it. An obstruction is just something to be navigated. They don't take roadblocks personally. If they did, Harald never would have navigated the chairs and objects designed to keep him in the kitchen as a puppy. And if he hadn't made it past the makeshift fence, he would have never made his way to his favorite snuggle spot on my husband's feet. A roadblock is not personal. When we hit a wall, instead of trying to negotiate it, we often try to figure out what its message is or what it has to do with how we are in the world. Dogs just look at obstacles as the next thing to overcome. From now on, I'm just going to pretend to be Harald when roadblocks show up!

Expansion

I ran into a computer glitch the morning after writing about persistence. I was working on my laptop while on vacation. I was able to get an internet connection for a while, but quickly lost it. Then I was able to open a Word document, but not type into it. Finally, I used Notepad. Persistence won out. I noticed how often the things I write about show up in my life shortly after writing about them. And I realized that at other times, the things that need to show up in my writing appear in my life first, before I write about them. That morning, I recognized the dance I was doing with my writing; I noticed my rhythm.

When I started working as an activities director at a nursing home, for the first three months I kept saying, "I can't find my rhythm." I felt both off balance and faltering in my activities. I seemed to keep starting and stopping things. This was actually true. Whether I was charting, leading a movement group, or in a meeting, there were constant interruptions.

I needed to find a way to incorporate the interruptions into what I was doing. As a group leader, this was relatively easy. I expanded the field I was working with. I held multiple groups in my awareness at the same time: the residents participating in the group and the nurses and attendants who walked in with medications during a group. On occasion, I asked the nurses and attendants to move or play with us—which deterred some from ever interrupting again. Often, I just took a breath and knew that even the interruptions were part of the dance. Eventually, I was able to accept the interruptions as part of my job, not a distraction from it.

Instead of behaving as if certain people and things are not supposed to be where they are, we can see all of life as one integrated dance and everything that shows up in the moment as part of that dance. If we approach every desired outcome in this same way, we might recognize that we are always moving towards that desired outcome, whether we appear to be taking the "right" steps or not. This is different from magical thinking, which is believing that the universe will do the work. Rather, it is holding a perspective that apparent distractions are part of the path while, at the same time, keeping your energy and awareness on the outcome you want. Instead of being annoyed that the dog wants a walk, I can see that walk as an integral part of my writing—without knowing how my writing will be affected.

This awareness energetically keeps you moving in the direction you want and wards off feelings of frustration and despair that can lead to giving up and feeling stressed. You can think of desired outcomes the same as physical destinations. You have to traverse miles to arrive at your destination, but you allow yourself to enjoy the scenery along the way. Appreciating the sights doesn't mean you aren't still headed in the direction you've chosen. The expansion of awareness takes no time, so you can bank your thirty seconds. But if you'd like a 30-second play break, try this.

30-Second Play Break

Stop what you are doing and breathe in deeply and allow all thoughts outside of the tree (or any object) in front of you fall to the wayside for thirty seconds.

Compassion

Compassion was the word that went on Ashley's angel card. Ashley is my oldest stepdaughter, and at the time I created the cards, she was a little challenging for me. The picture on the card was of the two of us. My arms were wrapped around her and we both looked serene and happy. The words I put on the card were, "I can embrace all of me." I saw me embracing myself as I did Ashley, even my challenging aspects.

Compassion goes hand in hand with gentleness, with one often evoking the other. But as with gentleness, many of us are able to employ compassion for another, but have trouble feeling it for ourselves. Somehow, we believe we are unique and should be living to higher standards than others. We don't offer the same words of encouragement or feel the same sympathy we would for others in a difficult situation.

I find this most extreme with clients who have been physically, emotionally, or sexually abused as children, and who still believe as adults that they did something wrong to deserve the abuse. They may believe there is something inherently wrong with them and, therefore, they cannot show themselves any compassion. But the abused do not have a monopoly on this condition. Most of my clients can be very compassionate towards others but have a limited or nonexistent supply for themselves.

Why should you be compassionate towards yourself? For some, it is obvious: it feels better. Others fear that if they stop cracking the whip and alleviate their own suffering, nothing will ever get done. They believe only negative motivators work.

As mentioned earlier, I see this often in my therapy practice. We use scare tactics with ourselves (and often with others) to get the job done. While scare tactics may work, they don't tend to get the best results. If I am writing from a place of fear, I may be rushing, censoring, and/or skipping important information. Fear will not bring out the best material. Take the path that creates the least resistance and evokes the most fun. That's what I say!

As an added bonus, it has been shown that people who practice compassion produce more DHEA (the antiaging hormone) and less cortisol (the stress hormone).[9] Compassion will keep you young longer.

Detachment

The ability to consciously distance oneself from what is happening in the moment is sanity preservation. When things appear to be chaotic or maybe just going in a different direction than you would choose, you need to be able to find your own center, which connects you to your heart and rational thinking. It is way too easy to get caught in whatever spins of energy are occurring in the moment.

Many years ago I worked with a woman named Charlotte who came in for her appointment very upset about the inappropriate behavior of her daughter's friends in her home. She had become enraged by their disrespect. As we sorted through her feelings, one thing became clear to me: Charlotte was unaware that she didn't have to get upset, even when people around her were behaving badly. She could have stayed calm, said, "I'm going to ask you to leave my house now," and left it at that. Her eyes became wide when I presented this as an option.

Though most of us know we can choose whether to let these types of situations get under our skin, we often don't act as if we have a choice. Practicing a little detachment will give us some space to decide how we would like to respond (not just react).

Sometimes we need tricks to help us detach. By far the most common—and probably simplest—is to become conscious of your breathing and count to ten (in the space of thirty seconds). That works sometimes. If that's not working, you might imagine the scene in front of you as if it is on a movie screen. Pretend you are sitting with a bucket of popcorn, totally entranced, wondering how the movie is going to unfold. Or if the person in front of you is someone who consistently pushes your buttons, imagine them as some fictional villain, like the Wicked Witch of the West in *The Wizard of Oz*, or imagine yourself as the Buddha or Mother Teresa.

These brief moments of detachment will help you come back to your adult, competent self, and every situation will be easier to handle.

Wondering

Have you ever looked at a couple walking down the street and wondered how long they've been together? Where they met? What their lives are like? Have you ever hiked up a mountain or hill and wondered what was on the other side? Have you walked a city street, passed a pharmacy, and wondered if anyone lives above it?

I used to live in New York City and once wondered what would happen if the ground under my feet split open. Does that seem like a morbid thought to you? It wasn't to me. I just had a moment of knowing that the things we take for granted or assume to be solid are not necessarily so. And I didn't panic or freak out, I just wondered what that experience would be like. I had fun by stepping outside of what we call reality and into the unknown.

When I first visited Santa Fe, I felt a strong pull to live there. I wondered what my life would look like and if I would be happy living there. I didn't try to figure it out, I just enjoyed the fantasy.

When you let yourself wonder about the unknown, it creates an opening for exploration. You know that you are playing in the world of imagination where there are no right or wrong answers. You allow yourself to create things, to make things up. No one will know and no one will care.

But way too often, we cut wonder off before we've explored its riches. Instead of wondering if I'll ever be married, I try to figure out where he is and when he is going to show up. Instead of wondering what my life might look like in Santa Fe, I start desperately trying to find a job and a home to see if I can make it work. Action steps, which may be necessary in the future, can be premature. When they are, they can prevent us from diving into the realm of possibility.

This is like brainstorming ideas with a group of people and having someone (there's always at least one) in the group who can't abide to the brainstorming rule of withholding judgment. They either immediately see drawbacks to an idea or try to figure out how to make an idea work. And if the person can't immediately see how to make an idea work, they dismiss it. This behavior sucks the energy out of the brainstorming session and no further ideas flow from the participants. Everyone needs to give the initial chaos of brainstorming enough space to move and create. The time for seeing if an idea will actually work comes later.

When my husband and I were planning our marriage, we didn't have a lot of money and didn't think we could afford a honeymoon. So we did what I hope everyone does in that situation, we created a vision board (a visual representation or collage of the things they want to have, be, or do in life). We asked ourselves where we most wanted to go. I was torn between Alaska and Hawaii; he really wanted to go to Hawaii. We created a board with beautiful pictures of luaus, oceans, leis, and all other things Hawaiian. Then we put it where we could see it. Soon we heard of a wedding fair in Santa Fe, and the grand prize for attendees was a trip to Hawaii. I thought to myself, *Yes, this is it, we're going to win.*

Gail, a little smarter than me in that moment and curiously able to read my mind, said, "Let go, you can't control it."

Well, I didn't let go and we didn't win the trip. I had no idea how we were going to get our honeymoon. By default, I let go and entered into wonder. The next day, I received a phone call from my big brother who said this to me, "Mel, we don't have a lot of money, but we want to do something nice for your wedding. How about our frequent flyer miles? We have enough to get both of you to either Hawaii or Alaska, your choice."

It was magic, pure and simple—the kind of magic that sometimes happens when you release expectation of outcome or the desire to control and just allow yourself to step into wonder.

When we wonder, we give the universe room to work. When we try to control or figure things out in our minds, we contract and limit possibilities. Next time you feel stuck on a problem, stop for thirty seconds and just allow yourself to gaze out the window or at a picture on the wall. Giving your mind a momentary pause may help you to see new options.

Imagination

Imagination and wonder are often used synonymously, but in my mind, they are slightly different. When I am asked to use my imagination, it feels like I am searching for a solution. Maybe it goes back to my own programming. When I was growing up, I was often told or heard said, "Use your imagination." But there is also something inherently wrong with that admonition. It gives me ownership of imagination, as if it were something that belonged to me. Perhaps it's really the opposite. What if imagination does not *belong* to any of us but, instead, can be *tapped into* by each of us?

When I try to imagine, it feels like I am working at it. My fondest memories of imagining are as far from work as one could imagine. Ha! The two most vivid memories come to mind.

The first was when I did a twenty-four-hour vision quest in the Colorado Rockies. I was on my own, with nothing but water, a journal, and a lip balm. (Never go anywhere without lip balm in Colorado.)

I had lots of time to play. If you've never been on your own for twenty-four hours in the wilderness, I can tell you that it is a completely different experience of time. One minute felt like at least ten; an hour like an eternity. I was confined to the safe place I had created around me, just slightly larger than my body stretched out to its full length. Exploring the area was not an option, so I lay on my back and looked up.

Lucky for me, there were lots of clouds moving across the sky that day. As I watched the clouds, many of my loved ones who had passed on formed a parade. I saw my father, my first dog, my dear friend John, and others. In the moment, it didn't feel, even a little bit, like I was imagining them. It felt like they were visiting. I was deeply moved by the experience. When we truly drop into the experience of imagining, it becomes hard to distinguish it from reality. That's why visioning can be so powerful.

My other memory of imagining was at Carlsbad Caverns National Park in New Mexico. The caverns are famous for their stalagmites and stalactites, which are naturally occurring mineral formations. I was stunned by their beauty as I walked through the massive caves. I stopped at one spot, looked across the way, and saw the face of a beautiful gypsy-like woman in the stalactites. I studied her a while, but when I turned away to tell my friend to look at her, she disappeared. No matter how many angles I looked from, I couldn't find her again. Was she real or imagined?

As I talk about these two powerful memories of imagining, I see that what they have in common is that I wasn't *trying* to imagine anything. By allowing myself to sit in the beauty and the mystery, things started appearing in my awareness.

When we talk about imagining something, we are trying to capture a naturally occurring response to being open. Wonder can take us into that open space where imagining spontaneously starts to happen.

So, now using our imagination has a whole different spin.

Research by neuroscientists into the brain's plasticity and ability to constantly reshape itself also informs us that the brain does not distinguish between a "real" experience and a vividly "imagined" experience. In an oft-cited study done at Harvard in 1994, two groups of volunteers repetitively played a five-fingered combination of notes on a piano. They did this for two hours a day for five consecutive days, while another group just imagined playing and hearing the same sequence of notes for the same duration of time. At the end of the five days, brain scans showed that the finger maps for the volunteers who had played the notes had grown as expected, but, remarkably, the maps for the volunteers who had just imagined playing them had also grown to the same extent.[10]

Athletes and coaches in all sports and countries are very practiced in visualizing peak performance. We can easily translate this skill into every area of our lives. We can allow ourselves to enjoy the imagining that occurs spontaneously and know that it has the potential to transform. Maybe we should take wonder breaks instead of coffee breaks.

The habits of gentleness, curiosity, persistence, expansion, compassion, detachment, wondering, and imagination are gateways to an easier, less stressful life. They are not necessarily things to do in thirty seconds or less. Rather, they are more a way of being in the world that invites joy and easy flow. That said, you could set an alarm to go off on the hour and take thirty seconds to reflect on any of these qualities. Those thirty seconds will go a long way towards turning these qualities into habits that occur without thinking, and your life may effortlessly feel easier.

6

Play for Health

Imagination, curiosity, and wonder are qualities that naturally occur in play—which may be the most underrated resource we have available.

You know (I hope) that play and relaxation are good for your health, but play is also great for relationships and productivity. Our relationships improve with play. It follows that better relationships create less stress and even help mitigate the effects of stressful events. If you stop for a moment to reflect on the times in your life when you were truly productive, you might notice that it didn't feel like you were working hard. Maybe you were even having fun.

In his best-selling book, *Flow*, Mihaly Csikszentmihalyi describes a natural state of being that is not only enjoyable, but highly productive: flow.[11] The flow state is harmonious and effortless, and whether you are performing a mundane task or climbing a mountain, the experience is one of optimal personal satisfaction. The flow state is also nonresistant. We are so engaged, we often don't notice the passage of time. Flow can be found while hiking, dancing, dining with friends, writing a book, or being on an assembly line. It is both a state of mind and a feeling state in the body. The mind is nonresistant; the body is alert and aware of sensation. When in a state of flow, we feel alive and in tune with what is going on inside us while also feeling in tune with what is happening in our environment.

In Flow Climbing a Mountain, In Flow Baking Bread

Sometimes the flow state occurs spontaneously. You wake up in a good mood and find it easy to go with the flow, quite literally. (I love those days.) But there are many things you can do to encourage flow when you're not feeling it. Everything covered in this book supports flow. Learning to move through thoughts, feelings, and habits that limit flow can be the first step in restoring natural flow. Being gentle with yourself. And using the other supportive habits already discussed can be seen as coaxing the flow state.

But let's explore how play goes beyond coaxing and actually takes us into this highly productive and enjoyable way of being in life.

My definitions of play and flow merge together. Any activity that allows me to be in the moment brings me into a state of openness. From this open state, I can play with thoughts, objects, art materials, music—anything. It is the place of creativity. Nothing gets stuck or becomes solid.

One of the ways I was able to stay in the moment and be playful with my writing was to imagine the words bouncing around on the page. *Play with the words. Words with the play. With the words play. Would that I would.* I am also in the habit of keeping toys on my desk, stopping for a wrestle with the dog, and singing familiar tunes with made-up words when I feel stuck. All of these activities help me stay present and focused with the task at hand, not the opposite, as some might believe.

In our society, play is not simply a four-letter word; it is often considered a four-letter word of the indecent variety. It is an activity and state of mind that most relegate to the bottom of the priority list. The value of play is forgotten or dismissed.

When I first began working with a business coach, many years ago, I was asked to rank various items from one to twenty-five, in order of their importance to me. The list included things like relationships, work, church, children, play, and ethics. Most items were easy to rank, but play and relationships were not. Which came first for me? I finally decided on play because for me, play is the highest spiritual place in which I can find myself. Play is a state of mind that means I am relaxed, at ease, willing, curious, flexible, and in joy. If I am in a playful state of mind, my relationships are easier. So relationships came second on my list and everything else followed.

When I got the analysis of my personality type and business challenges based on my rankings, I was stunned. The report said I didn't care about people and used words along the lines of lazy and unmotivated. It certainly didn't match the way I saw myself. I checked with the people who knew me well and would be honest with me. They were equally shocked and assured me that this was not an accurate picture. When I went back to the coach and explored this, it was revealed that putting play at the top of my list was what drove the analysis. Though I continued to work with this coach for a few months, I never felt that she got it—or got me.

People are more productive, have better relationships, and are healthier when they are having fun. Ashley Montagu, British-American anthropologist and humanist, believed we are designed to play, designed to maintain many aspects of our childlike nature.

Montagu and others before him (Bolk, DeBeer, Lorenz, Gould) identified human beings as neotenous creatures. Neoteny is the quality of staying young longer in form and function. The physical retention of childlike traits was postulated by Montagu, Bold, DeBeer, Lorenz, and Gould to translate into psychological traits. This means that humans are designed to maintain childlike qualities into adulthood. And at the top of the list of childlike qualities is play.

As adults, we have forgotten how to have fun. We have replaced movement and laughter with eating and alcohol. Statistics on job and life dissatisfaction, depression, and stress are at all-time highs. But we *can* have fun while we work, and having fun will add to our productivity and performance. Play fosters curiosity, trust, resilience, and awareness. It enhances creativity and flexibility. It was a tool used by Benjamin Franklin, Thomas Edison, and Carl Jung. Don't you want to play?

30-Second Play Break

Turn this book upside down and let four or five words jump out at you. Take your words and make a sentence. One that has meaning or not. Any sentence will do.

I define play as an open, unattached way of interacting with self, others, or objects: spontaneous being. But if you were to ask one hundred people for a definition of play, you would likely get an equal number of unique definitions ranging from gambling to wasting time to being in the flow of life with God.

Play is a very personal experience. Its definition has been individually shaped for each of us, and we each have a different internal response when invited to play. Some minimalize, demean, devalue, and trivialize play; others (like me) exalt it as the highest of activities.

Webster's New World Dictionary has fourteen definitions for play as an intransitive verb, nineteen definitions for play as a transitive verb, nine as a noun, and another nineteen definitions for common play phrases, such as play along with, or play for time. The definitions include gambling, acting, amusing oneself, deceiving others, imitation, moving lightly, sports, fun, and joking, to name a few.

Unfortunately, play has been corrupted for some by childhood experiences where the word play was used inappropriately. Bullies of all sorts may have said, "We're just playing," or, "This will be our secret game," leaving the victim confused about play. That often results in the victim hating play in all its forms.

The good news is the antidote is play itself! When we allow ourselves to play with past experiences and current challenges, we give ourselves permission to rearrange perceptions and beliefs about ourselves. Play allows us to take risks, test out new options, try on new characters, and do things upside down and backwards. Simply engaging in playful activities encourages resiliency and healing.

I frequently use joking and laughter—two forms of play—in the therapeutic process. Besides being a great relationship builder, laughter is like a mudslide, pulling things no longer needed away, allowing limiting beliefs and stuck feelings to easily dissolve.

Play fosters creativity and flexibility. It also brings us into relationship with others. Research has shown that play triggers the secretion of serotonin and endorphin (chemicals associated with pleasure, reward, and stress reduction). Inviting play into our adult lives can both momentarily and permanently change our perspectives on life. By taking ourselves a little less seriously, we can loosen our grip and remember what it's like to have fun.

Brian Sutton Smith, PhD, professor emeritus of psychology at the University of Pennsylvania, says that the opposite of play is not work, but depression.[12] When we don't incorporate play into our lives, we lose the joy life has to offer. Our physical, mental, emotional, and spiritual health are at risk for disease—that is, lack of ease.

Resistance to Playing and Counteracting It

Many adults resist playing, and for many good reasons. Play has been judged harshly by our work oriented society. Many of us have grown up being told, "Stop playing around and get back to work," "There's no time to play," "Aren't you ever going to grow up?" and, "You're acting like a child." We have also been told there's a right and wrong way to play, and there's a time and place (which never seems to be here or now) to play.

In every workshop I've ever done, there is a quiver in the room when I say, "Let's play." For some it's a quiver of excitement; for many it's the quiver of anxiety that is aroused when they feel they may be put on the spot or embarrassed. I always let participants know all activities are optional. Just because I think something is fun doesn't make it so for everybody.

Because of its very nature, play often asks us to step out of our comfort zone and risk feeling foolish. We are afraid of losing control, making mistakes, being compared to others, and failing. We use the excuses of being too tired, too old, and too busy to play. Almost every impediment to play revolves around fear. And most of that fear is imagined. When you are playing in a group with others, it is highly unlikely anyone is paying close attention to you. They are too engaged in their own play. And by its very nature, play embraces everything as part of the activity. What you think is foolish, others may consider brave.

Why break through the resistance? When we allow ourselves to take play breaks, even small ones, or play with whatever is showing up in this moment, we are pausing the programs and beliefs that typically drive our behavior. When I pause to play with an object on my desk, curiosity is evoked. I feel a sense of spaciousness in my body and a desire to share my findings with someone. But just reading about it doesn't give you the felt sense in your body. So, let's practice.

30-Second Play Break

If there's a toy nearby, use that. If not, just pick up any object and pretend it's a toy. See how it moves, and what it's designed to do. Then do something different with it. Pretend you don't know what it's supposed to do or try doing it the opposite way.

What do you notice in your body? What thoughts do you notice?

In just a moment, we can shift our state of awareness. We all know what a one-week vacation can do for us. We might think of playing in the moment as a way of taking that vacation and chunking it down into bite-size experiences that we can embed into our daily routines. What if we measured play as an activity of daily living, as important as brushing our teeth?

Prescribing thirty seconds of play every hour might improve the health of any practitioner's clientele. And play is one preventive treatment anyone can self-prescribe.

Rules and Play

When we play sports and board games, there are rules we agree to follow. The rules provide structure and help participants feel safe to engage. They know what is expected of them and what they can expect from others. In professional football, a player knows that another cannot pull on his helmet without incurring a penalty for the team (if the referee catches it). When playing Monopoly, the Go to Jail (and do not collect $200 dollars) card gives us a very specific direction to follow. In football, the destination is the goal line; in Monopoly, the purpose is to amass money and real estate.

But play doesn't always have rules. Dancing at a rock concert, splashing in the ocean, and building a fort are play behaviors that don't need rules or a specific outcome. These types of play are of a more open and spontaneous nature.

In spontaneous play, creativity abounds. We don't know what's coming next. This is crucial for inventors in any field. But the more structured aspects of play support bringing things into form. All artists need both skills to bring their art to fruition. The same can be said of life. Balancing spontaneity and creativity with structure and organization allows us to bring our uniqueness into the world with integrity.

Many group activities naturally incorporate both aspects of play, providing enough structure to allow for spontaneous action. Most people enjoy these games. They are given the opportunity to take risks at a comfortable level. As with playing the stock market, we all have different risk comfort levels to be honored.

There are many different ways we play: games, art, music, words, sports, puzzles, sex, and imagination, to name a few. Within each of these categories of play, we will find activities that are organized and structured and others that are free-form and without rules.

One of the benefits of play is that it can help us restore balance between spontaneity and organization in our lives. Leaning too far in either direction is an unidentified stressor for many people. If your life is exceedingly organized in every area, you may feel that life is joyless and all work. You may take everything seriously and feel trapped, uninspired, and uncreative. On the other hand, if your life is without structure and order, you may feel lacking in purpose or out of control. You may have lots of great ideas that never take form and find it difficult to work with a team.

Sometimes we unconsciously correct these imbalances. If you work at a job where you are expected to be very organized, you may keep a messy home. If you are an artist with an ever-changing schedule, you may bring structure into your life through the way you take on small tasks.

Play gives us an opportunity to consciously restore balance by choosing activities to loosen up something that has become too fixed or organized or by showing us how to organize disparate resources and bring creativity to form. One easy way to bring organized play to a messy desk is to use boxes of different shapes and color to sort papers and supplies. If your desk is always perfectly arranged, there should be open space to put a toy of your choosing in an easy to reach spot. Then you just have to remember to turn the toy upside down and backwards every so often.

Time and Ways to Play

As you may have just discovered in the above play exercise, play does not have to be time-consuming. You can embed play activities into everything you do, and you can think of play as a state of mind, even if you are sitting in a meeting with your boss. Imaginative play comes in quite handy. Whether you love your boss or hate your boss, imagining that you are having the conversation with him (or her) on a lounge chair by a pool will create more relaxation in your body. If you do, in fact, feel challenged by your boss, using the technique of imagining him as a cartoon character might make it easier to digest what is being said.

Here is a list of ways you can play in your office, home, clinic, or store to get you started.

1. Place windup toys in strategic places and use them when you are stressed.
2. Use your senses as play signals. For example, you shimmy every time you hear a phone ring.
3. Create wonderful smells in the office.
4. Use office equipment as candy bowls.
5. Wash with sound. Imagine the music is bathing every cell of your body.
6. Create a sound barrier; put your own words to a familiar tune.
7. Play with your food. How many shapes can you carve into your sandwich?

8. Take five-minute fun breaks. Dance to music, write a poem (say, in the style of Dr. Seuss), give a dance lesson to a friend (no skills needed), daydream, wear an outrageous item of clothing, give yourself or someone else a massage, or meditate.
9. Have chair races—the best thing you will ever do with an office chair.
10. Call someone and pay them a compliment.
11. Read two pages of a Calvin and Hobbes book every hour.
12. Take scheduled vacation breaks in your mind.
13. Recite silly poetry in your mind (or out loud to willing coworkers or customers).
14. Be Rhett Butler, John Wayne, or Lady Gaga for one minute or as long as you can maintain it.
15. Play kitchen hockey in the break room—with spatulas and food.
16. Make up a secret code or language with a coworker.
17. Dream up a new flavor of chewing gum.
18. Make a sculpture with objects on your desk.
19. See how tall a tower you can build with office supplies.
20. Knock it down.
21. Hum along to the sounds in your workplace.
22. Make funny faces to the annoying client on the phone.
23. Build something using only marshmallows and spaghetti.
24. Intentionally create a drama out of the littlest annoyance, just for your own enjoyment.
25. Bounce in your seat.
26. Use different colored pens to match your mood.

27. Howl at the moon.
28. Make funny faces at yourself in the mirror.
29. Pick a task and do it exactly as your mother or father would have done it.
30. Move like a zombie.

7

Using Your Body's Wisdom

Almost four years ago, my husband and I moved the location of our clinic. The first six months were pretty slow for my practice. I had not replaced the clients who chose not to continue because of the distance. And then I started dancing. Within two or three weeks of being in dance class, moving my body, restoring flexibility and movement to my joints, my practice was full. This experience demonstrated a concept we will be exploring in this chapter: Where the body goes, mind and life will follow.

One thing we all have in common is a body, and whether we love it or hate it, we're not going anywhere without it. To say that we take it for granted is a gross understatement for many of us. If you don't stop to think about what a valuable tool your body is, your unconscious mantra can quickly become use it and abuse it. Sure, we know it has hands that can type and feet that can walk, but most of us were not taught that how we move and breathe can affect our relationships, our health, and, metaphorically, how we move through the world.

In previous chapters, we looked at how awareness and sensation, along with the mind, can support letting go of thoughts, feelings, and behaviors. We also looked at behaviors that can be used to support well-being and relieve stress, including play. Now we will see how the body can, quite literally, show us how to be in the world in a more relaxed, open, and enjoyable way.

One Breath at a Time

It amazes me how often I forget the simplest and most effective tool I have available in every moment to effect change in perspective and mood: my breath.

The simple act of paying attention to the air as it comes in and leaves my body can settle me much more efficiently than anybody's words ever will. When I'm running around and trying to attend to other people's needs, my business, my dog, and many other things in my life, I sometimes forget what the priority is in the moment. In thirty seconds or less and with a simple breath, I can stop, re-center, and ask myself, "What is most important in this moment?"

Alexander Lowen, one of the pioneers in the field of somatic psychotherapy, speaks of how breath connects us to life in the following quote.

> The importance of breathing need hardly be stressed. It provides the oxygen for the metabolic processes; literally it supports the fires of life. But breath as "pneuma" is also the spirit or soul. We live in an ocean of air like fish in a body of water. By our breathing we are attuned to our atmosphere. If we inhibit our breathing we isolate ourselves from the medium in which we exist. In all Oriental and mystic philosophies, the breath holds the secret to the highest bliss. That is why breathing is the dominant factor in the practice of Yoga.[13]

Our first breath is the entry into life; our last is the exit from life. When we hold our breath, we stop engaging with the moment and with those around us. We also create tension in the body and prevent the natural flow of bodily fluids.

J. Heller and W. Henkin write that it is no wonder many diseases associated with old age are related to circulatory problems because we literally dry up.[14] The irony is that through our fear of living, we unconsciously bring on dying.

When something scares us, we hold our breath. If we are afraid of too much life, we inhibit our inhalation. If we are afraid of committing ourselves to life, we shorten our exhalation.[15] When we shorten the exhalation, we also prevent a complete letting go. I've seen myself and clients let go just a little, instead of fully letting go. I can watch this happening by observing the breath. There's a brief and short exhale. When we do not exhale fully, there is still something we're holding on to: stale breath, which does not support life. Without a full exhalation, there's no room for a full inhalation. This is not just a metaphor for life, it is life. When we can't fully let go with our breath, we don't create space in our bodies and lives for new things to come in.

Inhibiting the breath is another way we avoid feelings. I've seen many therapy clients talk rapidly with much resistance to my interrupting them and asking them to breathe. This is often an indicator that, for them, it's not safe to feel their feelings. When we slow down the speed of our thinking and speaking, we start to feel what is below the surface.

This can be scary at first.

When I first considered going to graduate school in Boulder, Colorado, my husband and I drove up one Thursday so I could sit in on a class or two at Naropa University. I liked the classes I visited, so I stopped at the admissions office to see about applying. The admissions guy, a very personable young man, chatted with me a few minutes, then said, "Well, you're going to interview this weekend, aren't you?"

I didn't know what he was talking about. It turned out to be one of two weekends a year that prospective students were invited to go through a rather intensive movement and verbal application process. The interviews started the very next day.

I left his office stunned. I went back to the hotel room, holding my breath the whole way, reeling from this information. Scared to get what I said I wanted, part of me was ready to get in the car and drive back to Santa Fe immediately. Instead, I allowed myself to breathe. Calls to friends and mentors for support were met by answering machines. What could I do? I got in bed, pulled the blankets over my head, and had a long and full crying episode.

The cool thing about crying full out is that it makes you breathe. During my meltdown, I created space in both my body and my life to have more. When I showed up for the interview the next day, I was ready to be accepted to the program.

We don't always get confronted with such a direct application of a principle.

But we all want something, and often when that something is offered to us, we get scared and hold our breath. When we *do* hold our breath, we inhibit our ability to engage and cut ourselves off from having what we want.

Besides being our direct, most immediate engagement with life, the inhalation and exhalation of breath can also teach us about flow and balance. If you feel out of flow or stuck, the conscious act of letting the breath move in and out, seeing it, and being fully aware of the circulation of oxygen in your system can help you feel flow in your body. The dance of the breath never stops, and when we become conscious of it, we can have some influence on how it flows. That, in turn, will impact the dance we do with life.

Conscious breathing is something we can do anyplace, anytime—even right now.

30-Second Play Break

This play break is a breathing break.

Pause and take three deep breaths, noticing the inhalation and the muscle tension required, the exhalation, the ease of letting go, and the moment of stillness between breaths. Play with the timing of the inhalation, the exhalation, and the space between breaths.

Tuning into the flow of your breath can also expand your awareness of how to flow with challenging situations in your life. Your breath can also restore your balance. If you are feeling overwhelmed, it's likely that your breath is more focused on the inhale, taking in too much without letting enough out. On the other hand, when you feel you have nothing left to give, you may find that you are breathing out fully but inhibiting your inhalations. This correlates to giving and receiving. When we are unable to receive, there is a shortened inhalation and we find ourselves depleted, without energy.

Another way to play with breath as a metaphor for life is to watch the beginning, middle, and end of the inhalation and exhalation. Not only will you balance your breathing by watching it in this way, you will start to tap in to the natural rhythm of life. Everything we experience as human beings has a beginning, middle, and end. Like breath, the complete cycle could be less than a minute, or like birth and death, it could span a lifetime. The first act of breathing for a newborn is an inhalation. And at any given time in our lives, we are at the beginning of some adventures, in the middle of others, and coming to completion with still others. And like the breath, if there is an imbalance, we are likely to feel a little off center.

If we have six new projects starting simultaneously, we are likely to feel overwhelmed, correlating to too much inhalation, not enough exhalation. We may find ourselves taking frequent but incomplete inhalations, as if the speed of breathing will give us a better start. With nothing new and nothing completing, everything moving steadily along, we might feel bored or antsy. Stuck in the middle of the breath, we may not be allowing either a full inhalation or full exhalation and feel resistant to the stillness in between breaths. When we are completing a project, we may naturally express the ending with long, extended exhalations or sighs. These may express satisfaction or relief that we are done at last.

When we are in situations that ask us to be doing many things at once, it is imperative that we remember to exhale consciously. Taking thirty-second breathing breaks throughout your day can help restore rhythm, ease, and flow to your life.

Employ the Senses

The senses are another great tool always available to support self-care. When I was the activities director in a nursing home, I was bombarded daily by invasive sights, sounds, and smells. To soothe my nervous system and those of the residents I worked with, I offered groups that incorporated music, cooking, walks outside, and other activities, all designed to feed the senses in a nourishing way.

Sometimes we naturally gravitate towards a compensatory experience for the senses. After leaving a loud party, we might head to a quiet place to talk, or after riding a roller coaster, we might choose to sit for a while.

As a human being, you relate to the world through your senses, and the senses can be employed to evoke great pleasure or great pain. When you pay attention to the senses, you are paying attention to this moment. Seeing, feeling, tasting, hearing, and touching only happen here and now.

Many people visualize what they want in their mind's eye or even through a vision board. I keep my vision board hanging above my computer monitor. It serves as a tangible reminder of the things I want in my life. So when I look up and see the image of my "kick-ass body," it reminds me that I might not really want a piece of candy. When I see happy pictures of myself with my husband in London, I remember that travel is a priority for me. When I see pictures of the ocean and dancers, these are reminders of the state of mind I aspire to.

Surrounding yourself with pictures and photographs of the things that soothe your senses may support your well-being without your even actively looking at them. The subconscious is always registering the environment faster than thinking and impacting well-being in either a positive or negative way. Learn to use this to your advantage.

We are all wired to receive and use sensory input from birth. This is why we see infants trying to put everything (and anything) in their mouths. They want to employ every sense they have as a way to explore, process, and understand new information. There is much written about allowing children to learn through experience, not just lecture. It is generally agreed that children need to use their senses and be engaged in meaningful experiences. Not only does this early exploration with the senses form neural sensory pathways, it also helps them hone their senses.

Most adults forget what they once did naturally as children. When we engage our senses, we are more apt to learn and retain, better and faster. With this skill, starting a new job is automatically less stressful, meeting new people is easier, and transitions of all kinds can happen with less angst.

In this digital age, it is all too easy to lose track of our environment and the sensory experience. A walk in the woods doesn't automatically mean communing with nature. We may be talking, texting, or rocking out to the music on our headsets rather than experiencing the forest around us. The transition time we used to have when flying may now be filled with computer work, and the transition time we used to have when driving may now be filled with phone calls.

Good chefs know that we eat with all our senses. We want our food to taste good and feel good texturally *as* we eat it. We want it to smell and look good *before* we eat it, and sometimes we even want it to sound good (think of the crunch of a potato chip). With all the senses engaged, no wonder eating is so pleasurable for most of us.

The more senses we employ, the more engaged we are in an experience. Paying attention to sensation can be seen as the antidote to resistance, asking us to be present for every moment. And even though there are many moments in our lives when we might prefer to escape, the approach that is easiest on the body is to be with what is right here, right now.

30-Second Play Break

For ten seconds, stop and listen. What sounds are you hearing? For your next ten seconds, look around, what are you seeing? And in your final ten seconds, what do you feel in your body?

Combining Breath and Sensation

One of the body's natural responses to stress is to contract or tighten the muscles. When we feel pressured by others or outside circumstances, we pull into ourselves to get away from the external. This strategy for handling stress makes sense in theory, but in practice, it results in feeling like there is no space to be, which results in being easier to push around. And that makes you more vulnerable.

I often have my clients experience this by having them stand and just think about wanting to get away. They naturally contract and pull in. Then I give them a gentle push (with their permission, of course), and they inevitably lose their balance. When I ask them to let go of the resistance and contraction, then try to push them with the same force, they either easily stand their ground or flow back easily if they lose balance a little.

30-Second Play Break

Find someone to help you feel what I have just described in your own body. Help them experience it, too, by taking turns (thirty seconds at a time) being the subject (the one who receives the push) and the experimenter (the one who gives a slight push when the subject first thinks about wanting to get away and again when they release resistance).

We want to feel our power, not lord it over others. We want to be able to stand our ground and feel confident. That is the antithesis to stress. Catching the contraction in your attitude and body takes practice and awareness, but it will help you stand in your own center instead of collapsing to the will of others or unconsciously trying to have power over them.

First, simply set an intention to notice how often this happens. Whether there are many demands on your time, someone is verbally attacking you, or the roof is falling in, just notice the tendency of the body to contract. Then, as you start catching this sooner, just start adding a breath, one that includes a full inhalation and exhalation. Imagine opening and dropping down into the body.

If you think you don't know how to do this, remind yourself that it is what you do every night in order to fall asleep. As you breathe and open, pay attention to sensation: how your breath feels moving in and out of the body, the air on your arms, any tightness in your neck or shoulders. And just keep imagining that you are opening inside, creating room for yourself.

We also have a tendency to contract around internal discomfort. The contraction goes hand in hand with resistance, almost as if the contraction could shut down the pain. Again, the strategy seems to make sense to the mind, but in practice, it holds the pain in. Is that really what you want to do? It can initially be pretty frightening to stop resisting pain because the general attitude is that if we don't resist pain, we will feel more pain.

You may want to practice on a mild headache or slight pain in the back, taking small steps into a new behavior. If you remember that the sensation you are experiencing is stuck energy and that you are keeping it stuck by contracting around it, you might be more willing to give it a try. When you open to the pain, you are giving it space to move. And contrary to what the mind believes, when the pain begins to move, it does not get bigger, it loosens and begins to dissolve.

Pay Attention

Within hours of writing the above section on employing the senses, I was out for a walk with my husband and our four-legged companion, Beatrice. We are lucky enough to live near the Platte River in a vibrant part of downtown Denver. While approaching the river, I looked up and saw a magnificent hawk.

I was so excited to see this hawk in my urban neighborhood that I stopped, took some pictures, and watched it until Beatrice became too impatient for us to stay any longer. But something else became apparent to me. No one around us was paying attention to the hawk. Had they seen it before and grown tired of it? Possibly, but I doubt it. Some were probably engaged in conversation; others in a hurry to get somewhere. But look what they missed!

Earlier, we looked at using awareness to interrupt the habits of overindulging. Let's revisit what awareness offers us and how it can be used to help minimize the effects of a busy life.

Awareness serves the function of interrupting our process of perception. Perception means taking hold of something from our external environment and making sense of it with our own personal files of meaning. Perception involves categorizing and filtering our sensations and sorting through what we perceive, then taking selected sensations and labeling them. We are very fast to categorize and filter our sensations, giving us the ability to dismiss much of what we encounter in every moment.

For example, I am walking down the street and I pass the bakery, the flower shop, and the liquor store. In less than a few seconds, I have compiled all the breads, cookies, pastries, cakes, chrysanthemums, roses, tulips, wine, vodka, beer, and gin into pastries, flowers, and alcohol. Very efficient. Categorizing and filtering can be wonderful tools for organizing, and even coping with overwhelm. If we didn't have the ability to filter, our minds would likely be unable to keep up.

But because of this automatic filter, we miss things, like the hawk. Awareness literally interrupts the process of filtering and categorizing midstream. It asks us to stop and pay attention to our surroundings, to see it as if we've never seen it before and don't know what it is.

When looking at a flower with awareness, we see its color and shape, we notice its aroma, and we might even touch it to get a sense of its texture. Without awareness, we see the flower, label it "flower," and keep going. While labeling is efficient, we miss the experience of being with the flower.

As clichéd as it sounds, I have asked clients to literally stop and smell the roses. The thirty seconds it will take to do this will *not* make you late to work, but *will* waken your senses and calm your nerves. No roses around? Take an extra moment to smell the aroma of the coffee you're already carrying as you walk from your car to the office or take an extra moment to feel your feet making contact with the ground. Less than thirty seconds to an expanded awareness of life.

Shaking and Bouncing

I love to shake! Shake my head, shake my shoulders, shake my booty. When I shake, things loosen up. The joints, the muscles, the thoughts, the feelings—everything. Bouncing and shaking gets me back in touch with my body and seems to reset my nervous system.

While I do this instinctively, there is strong evidence for shaking as a way to move trauma and release stress. Animals shake after surviving attacks, and shaking has been shown to bring cortisol (stress hormone) levels down. One side effect that is of particular interest is that when we bring our cortisol levels down, we reduce the desire to binge. Bingeing on food and alcohol, though possibly calming in the moment, wreaks havoc on the body and makes stress harder to deal with.

30-Second Play Break

To feel the power of shaking, just stop for a moment and shake your arms. You should immediately start to feel a loosening of your joints and muscles, and possibly your thoughts and emotions.

Shaking has the ability to reprogram physical, mental, and emotional holding patterns. And shaking is particularly good for the body's joints. (Did you know there are more than three hundred joints in your body?) Joints link the bones and provide mobility. No movement is possible without the joints. Synovial fluid covers the joints and serves to reduce friction. Like shaking a bottle of paint or nail polish before using to restore fluidity, we move the synovial fluid when we shake our bodies, and this creates more ease in our movement. When the joints are happy, we are more apt to want to get out of bed and do things. Happy joints support taking action. Taking action reduces stress.

Change Your Posture

I learned something about dogs a few years ago. A trainer we were working with suggested that when our lab mix, Beatrice, had her tail tucked because of perceived (but not real) threats, I could let her know that she was okay by lifting her tail. This signal from her body would remind her that she was safe. Really? I didn't know that! I did know that the tucked tail is my dog's body language for communicating that she is frightened. A confident, happy dog has her tail up in the air. The trainer explained that by lifting Beatrice's tail, her mind would receive the message that she was safe.

Guess what? It turns out that the same thing is true for us.

We not only hold and express emotions in and through the body, we also get signals from the body about how to feel. Without "knowing" this, I realize that I have *always* known this. I have been dancing since I was very young, and the awareness has been with me that different dance moves and positions affect my state of mind. Long before I studied to become a dance movement therapist, I was using movement for my own therapy.

Amy Cuddy, a social psychologist and Harvard University professor, has spent years studying the impact our body postures have on our moods. She has learned that how we stand impacts our hormones, specifically testosterone and cortisol. More testosterone translates roughly into more confidence. And more cortisol is associated with higher stress. Cuddy found that "high power poses" increase testosterone and inhibit cortisol, while "low power poses" do the opposite. Her research, done in collaboration with Dana Carney, found that just 120 seconds in a power pose was enough to increase testosterone by twenty percent and decrease cortisol by twenty-five percent. Changing your body posture has a biological impact on your brain. In her Ted talk, Cuddy demonstrates standing in the Wonder Woman power pose before a job interview or sales pitch.[16] As with power poses, the body has postures associated with every other feeling state.

What is the body posture that expresses joy and excitement in humans? It is eyes wide and bright, loud voice, perhaps bouncing, and sometimes pumping one's arms over the head. We expand our bodies when we express joy and excitement. What body posture communicates sadness or fear? Crouching, looking away, looking down, shrinking. We contract in when we communicate sadness or fear.

Here's an interesting fact: since 1988, we have seen a four hundred percent increase in the prescribing of antidepressants. Before 1988, few of us had personal computers. Before the 1990s, none of us spent time on the internet, Facebook, Twitter, Pinterest, YouTube, or LinkedIn. They didn't exist. And now a UN study shows that more people own cell phones than have toilets.[17]

Other factors are likely at play, but body posture is one that you have some control over. The body postures of being at the computer or texting on your cell phone is not one of joy. When we recognize that these postures are not what the body interprets as joy, we don't have to throw away our devices or quit our jobs. We can adapt practices of stretching, shaking, pumping our arms up in the air, or jumping to reset the system—in thirty seconds or less.

Smile

There are many studies about the impact smiling can have on our mood. Dr. Robert Zajonc, a psychologist at the University of Michigan proposed this theory in 1989: As certain facial muscles relax and tighten, they raise or lower the temperature of blood flowing to the brain. These changes in temperature, in turn, affect the activity of brain centers that regulate emotion. Research suggests that a cooler brain creates good emotions, while a warmer brain produces negative emotions. [18]

30-Second Play Break

Take a moment to put yourself in the posture that expresses joy and excitement. Open your eyes wide. Pick an upbeat word and say it in a loud voice. Bounce a little. Pump your hands over your head. Now add a second element: Smile.

The relationship you have with your body is the only one that will last your entire lifetime. It is worth exploring and nurturing. Who knows? One day your body might save your life.

8

Staying Inspired

Lack of inspiration is an unrecognized source of stress in our lives. It can also be the result of stress. It's the old dilemma: Which came first? Has lack of inspiration *caused* stress or *come from* it? Either way, when we feel uninspired, we carry ourselves differently and we interact with others in ways that do not support happy, healthy relating. We become less creative and eventually, everything feels like a burden. Let's look at some ways to keep your excitement for life fueled. Then let's see how to inspire others, because we all know that working around uninspired people is no fun either.

First Me, Then You

I am confident that when we are inspired, it's easy to be an inspiration to others. If we're not tapped in, we will quickly use up any reserves we might have. To serve others, we must first serve ourselves.

Besides the things that might be obvious in your life (for me, that includes meditation, dancing), there are many overlooked places to find inspiration. Two documentaries immediately come to mind: *Mad Hot Ballroom* and *Young at Heart.*

If you haven't seen these movies, put them on your list of must see movies. Start a special list of movies to inspire you.

Mad Hot Ballroom is a film by director Marilyn Agrelo and writer/producer Amy Sewell about a ballroom dance program offered in the New York City Public School system. The film follows fifth graders in three New York City neighborhoods as they learn the intricate dances of tango, foxtrot, swing, rumba, and merengue. Through dance, the children learn the skills they need to confront the challenges they face growing up. As I watched the film, I laughed, cried, and cheered all at once. I left the theater saying, "We need this program in Denver." And I'm pretty sure that if my life wasn't already maxed out and I had a clue where to begin, I would have brought that program to my city. Since I didn't, maybe someone reading this will.

I am inspired when I see lives being touched and transformed through movement. But dance doesn't have to be the vehicle for transformation. I actually decided to become a therapist after participating in transformational workshops in New Mexico with Judy Borich and Barbara Flood. While at those workshops, I recognized the great joy I got from witnessing others break free of the trauma and stories that made them feel less than whole. I wanted to be part of that movement! And while I don't get to see that in every session I facilitate, it often pops up to remind me why I do what I do.

Because we are busy and caught up with our jobs and lives, I think we often miss the impact we are having on others. Taking time out to reflect or even ask about how others' lives have been touched by your words or actions may give you pause. In the fast pace of the world today, it is way too easy to lose track of what is most important to us. And by the way, when I ask others, "What brings you the most joy?" the universal response is, "Being able to help others."

The other movie, *Young at Heart*, is another film that had a profound impact on me. After seeing it, I contemplated leaving everything behind to go join this rambunctious group of elders singing rock-and-roll hits. Not that I would sing; that wouldn't be pretty. But I did contemplate offering my limited choreography skills. Maybe I still will . . . someday.

Watching the rehearsals of this choir made up of men and women in their seventies and beyond touched my heart. Sharing the trials of aging, alongside the ecstasy of singing and community, gave me an appreciation for the fullness of life and the willingness to participate. Our degree of participation in what life presents is a key factor in our emotional well-being.

I have already spoken about what resistance does to us energetically in terms of keeping us stuck. Beyond letting go of resisting and allowing life to do what it does, we can actively step in and say, "Let's go for it!" As I contemplate doing something new, a sense of excitement and wonder automatically arise. And we know what excitement and wonder can do.

Inspiration from Within

We already know that external motivation only works temporarily, if at all. Internal motivation, or inspiration, is the flame within. It is interesting that the word is derived from the Latin *inspirare*, which has to do with breathing into. Of course, the word "inspired" is also often used in reference to being influenced by or on the receiving end of information from God or the gods.

Inspiration is a powerful force, and one we sometimes shy away from. If we feel inspired, we may have to take action. And sometimes that's the last thing we want to do. Knowing that there are times to seek inspiration and times to avoid inspiration, what follows are some of my favorite ways to find internal inspiration.

Do Something

Way too often, we stop ourselves from doing anything because we don't know what to do. We won't make a decision for fear of getting it wrong. Who cares? So what? Do it wrong. At least then you'll know and you'll be on your way to doing it right (if such a thing exists). I've seen this state referred to as "analysis paralysis." This is where our thinking gets us into serious trouble with sabotaging action (as talked about earlier). Don't listen to your mind. Just do it! This is a powerful concept. When you "do it," you are not only inviting the strong potential of feeling better about yourself, you are opening the door to seeing other possibilities. Heaven only knows how many mistakes I've made in the realm of investing in public relations, seminars, and coaching that have not paid in the way I hoped they would. Yet, there's not a one I didn't learn something from, even if it was never to do *that* again. One step leads to another. We can never be one hundred percent sure of a step until we take it, and all the trying to figure it out in advance is not going to change that.

Do Nothing

Yes, I'm contradicting myself. Sometimes the problem is that we are doing too much. We lose sight of what we're doing, why we're doing it, and what we'd rather be doing. At these times, it makes sense to stop and wonder. Don't think, just wonder. Let yourself get silent—meditate if you will—and listen. You may want to whisper a prayer to God, the universe, or whomever/whatever you ask for guidance and support. And then remember to let go.

Read a Favorite Book or Poem

There's nothing wrong with letting someone else's words inspire you. I have a couple of favorites that sit on my altar. I go back to them over and over again. You might even imagine that you are sitting with the author and having a conversation. What might he or she say to you in that moment? When you create that relationship with a book, you are honoring the author and giving and receiving simultaneously, whether or not the author is consciously aware of it.

Act as If You Are Already There

Imagine yourself as a best-selling author, world class athlete, or rock star at work. Acting as if it's already happened can create an internal feeling state that naturally motivates you. As you start thinking this way, you might notice that you sit a little more erect and there's more bounce in your step. Jack Canfield does a "Come as You Are in Five Years" party at his workshops and retreats. The participants are invited to come and tell stories of how their lives have unfolded and what their current experiences are (five years in the future). At the parties I've attended, people have shown up as newly engaged, carrying their best-selling book, wearing Olympic Gold medals, and demonstrating/talking about every other kind of desirable future you can imagine. This is how to use the mind, as opposed to letting the mind use you!

Replay Favorite Movie Scenes in Your Mind

The only drawback to this tip is that it involves having a good enough memory to find the scenes! Some of them may pop in easily, like Rocky Balboa running up the stairs at the Philadelphia Museum of Art. I think the music is what so strongly ingrains that scene in the memory. This is a good memory to call on when engaged in a physical activity that requires just a little extra push.

For long-term inspiration, I like Bill Murray in *Ground Hog Day*, doing the same thing over and over again. I love the freedom he finds, even in the despair. If you're going to be here forever and can't even manage to kill yourself, how many different ways can you do it? And in the end, the complete surrender, the peace that comes with giving up. And a new day begins.

The third scene that comes to mind is one I consider inspiring, though I admit that not everyone does: Cuba Gooding, Jr. shouting at Tom Cruise, "Show me the money!" in the film *Jerry Maguire*. His willingness to stand up, say what's true, and shout it at the top of his lungs takes chutzpah! When I need the courage to confront someone or something, this is a good memory to call upon.

Play Break

If you have begun a list of movies that inspire, add to it.

____

Anchor a Success Move in Your Body

Remembering someone else's success in your mind is great; remembering your own success in your body is even better. Neuro-linguistic programming (NLP) and Eye movement desensitization and reprocessing (EMDR) both have anchoring protocols. With each of these techniques, we're drawing on past experiences to recreate a feeling state in the body in the present moment.

In the NLP exercise, the first step is to remember a time when you had a success. It doesn't have to be big. Anything will do, even the first time your dog or cat went potty in the appropriate area. It doesn't matter what the success is so long as you consider it a success. Let yourself experience what you experienced in that moment: the pictures, the sounds, and the sensations.

I use a memory of something that happened when I was fifteen years old, on stage for a dance solo at a recital with hundreds of people in the audience. As I stood waiting for the music, I couldn't remember a single step. And then the music started and my body took over. I danced beautifully! At least that's the way I remember it. Over forty years have now passed since that recital, and I still remember the steps to that dance and hear the music in my mind. I use this memory to create a posture and a sound to anchor the feeling in my body. And now, each time I am in front of an audience or about to go into an important meeting, I can stop and find this posture and this sound to remind myself of what success feels like.

The EMDR process is a little different. You don't need a memory to begin. Instead, you think about how you would like to feel in the situation. Imagine performing or behaving in the way that is most powerful or comfortable for you, then notice how this feels in your body. Allow yourself to look for an image that supports this feeling. That image can be animal, vegetable, or mineral. If, for example, the feeling you want is peace and calmness, you might have an image of a mountain or an ocean to accompany it. Then imagine placing that image somewhere in your body where it would feel good to you. Putting the ocean in your legs might help you feel more fluid; putting a lion in your chest could support courage. See if there are any sounds or words that accompany the image. When you are in need of inspiration in the moment, you can call on your image and sounds to find that peaceful place. If, on the other hand, you want to feel powerful and energized, you might need a mother bear on your side. Just thinking about her growl empowers me!

Create Your Own Set of Flash Cards

In the chapter on supportive behaviors, I talked about the set of angel cards I made for myself. The same thing could be done with images from movies, quotes, poems, or photos to make your own personal inspiration deck. There are many decks of inspirational cards you could buy already packaged, but doing it yourself will ensure that every card has meaning to you.

Reconnect to What You Value

We all have certain core attributes we value. Examples of core values could include: learning, kindness, humor, authenticity, freedom, connection with others, play, peace, flow, justice, humility, spiritual devotion, and truth. These same values can be called on when you are in need of inspiration, no matter what the circumstances are. If resistance arises around any task, you can connect back to your core value of learning or your core value of flowing with what life presents. Or you can find the quality of humility in yourself needed to take on the task. It's easy to make a game of this. With whatever you are doing in the moment, find the connection to a value or quality you want more of in your life.

30-Second Play Break

Think about the time you are devoting to reading this book. How does reading this book align with what you value?

Move the Goalposts

Get crazy with your goals. One I like to play with is that when I am rich and famous (and thin) I'll be invited to participate in *Dancing with the Stars*! Outrageous images (and believe me, this is an outrageous image) can lighten us up and make the real goal seem much more attainable. If your goal is to be able to go home at the end of the day and not yell at the people you live with, imagine going way bigger. See yourself arriving home overflowing with love, kindness, and laughter. Imagine being awarded a gold star at the Olympics for your transformation. The crowd is cheering you on, and you know you are forever changed.

Pretend to Be Someone Else

This can be a really fun way to get things done. You can imagine spending the day, or just an hour, as your greatest hero or villain. If your mother was approaching the same task as you are attempting, how would she do it? What would Oprah do? Or your spouse or best friend? Think of someone who might fearlessly pick up the phone and make that call you've been afraid to make and pretend to be them. Or dress like the Buddha (however you would imagine he dressed) or Mother Teresa. My good friend Diane doesn't hesitate to talk to anyone, anytime, anywhere. Sometimes I pretend to be Diane. Let those people who you look up to and admire be role models you transform yourself into in your imagination.

Listen to Music and Books While Driving

This is probably the one downside for me of not commuting to work, because our home and clinic are at the same location. I used to play my favorite inspirational music while driving, and it had a big impact on my mood as I started my day. I also listened to Sedona Method™ releases, and even if I wasn't paying complete attention, they helped me get more centered and relaxed. Think about what you are listening to in your downtime. Does it support the state of mind you are trying to cultivate? As much as I love good funky music, it's not the best thing to have playing in the background when calm is what I need. And vice versa. Listening to new age hypnotherapy-type music is really not smart when I need energy. Pay attention to what you need and give that to yourself. And remember to make choices that support safe driving.

Others Have Gone before You

Sometimes we think we are a little too special. We forget that most of the challenges we face have been faced by others. I am particularly guilty of this when I have a physical ailment. It starts to feel very personal and even insurmountable. (And I'm not talking a life-threatening illness, I'm talking stubbed toes, the flu, a cold, or hot flashes.) It is meaningless to compare our ailments to those of others, but it is useful to recognize that you might be making a bigger deal out of the situation than is necessary. Ask yourself what you need and then let yourself have it.

Reduce the Intake of Negative Information

We often don't realize how much negative information we absorb in the form of fear, cynicism, and sarcasm. The media is highly slanted towards evoking feelings of fear and grief, and it may be affecting your mood in ways you are unaware of. There may also be people in your life who don't support and inspire you and, in fact, do the opposite. You may want to spend less time with them. Become a detective and start to watch for all the external input that doesn't serve you. Once you identify it, make a plan to do something different.

Let It Flow

I find that once I start down a path (in this case, the path of what inspires), new ideas keep popping up if I stay out of judgment of them as they arise. I get into a flow of looking for what's next and things I never would have thought of just start showing up. As in brainstorming, the key to letting this work for you is to refrain from judgment and avoid trying to figure out whether or not any particular idea will work.

This concept also comes into play when I write. Editing takes me out of flow. In the initial draft of anything I write—letter, e-mail, or book—I try to just let the inspiration flow. Later, I go back and edit for content, clarity, and typos.

Rejoice in the Discomfort

Often we get really uncomfortable when things are about to change for us, whether in a preferred or not preferred way. Recognize that the discomfort is a necessary first step for you before you take the leap, whatever it is. Find appreciation for the discomfort. Scenes from *The Wizard of Oz* and, in particular, the Wicked Witch melting, are popping into my head as I write this. What if your discomfort is your internal Wicked Witch showing her face, right before melting?

Remember What Is Waiting for You

Whether it's the personal feeling of satisfaction that comes from being in integrity with yourself or the juiciness of having money in the bank, getting in touch with how you expect to feel can be a powerful motivator. You might imagine seeing yourself burning your credit card bills after they've been paid off in full and how good that will feel. Or if there's something you don't want to face, remember the weight that will be lifted after you've dealt with it. If your goal is bigger than you (this ties back to values), envision how the world will be impacted by you when you reach it. That should get you going.

Quit or Give Up, Temporarily or Permanently

There are times to recognize that no matter what you do, you just can't find the motivation to keep going. This may be an indication that it's time to change directions or focus. In this case, quitting could save you a lot of time and energy.

But we sometimes feel like quitting even though we know we are on the right path. At those times, quitting for a day could be the best thing to do. A friend of mine who was very frustrated with her teenager told me she was going to take a break from being a mom for a month. I thought it was a great idea and suspected that everyone would feel better as a result.

Play Break

What can you take a vacation from for an hour, a day, or a week?

____

Hug Your Favorite Four-Legged Friend

I saved the best for last. When all else fails, go bury your head into the warm, fuzzy fur of your best friend. If you don't have one, borrow one. If you're allergic, buy a big stuffed animal. Whatever it takes.

Inspiring Others

We all take delight in knowing that we have inspired others, and most of us have opportunities to inspire others daily. Does a parent need inspiring to get involved in school activities? Is a mom struggling with an unmotivated teenager? Does a new supervisor need a boost in working with a team that lacks spirit? Once you've found your own inspiration, you will be able to lead others in a natural, inspired way.

Here are some ways to inspire others.

Give Them What They Need

As basic as it may sound, we often overlook this simple step in supporting others. There is nothing more frustrating than to be given a task that is impossible to complete because tools or information are missing. To ask one of your children to clear the snow but not give them a shovel or ask an employee to call the printer without providing the printer's name is setting them up for failure and feelings of disempowerment and frustration.

Situations will uniquely define what is needed based on the people involved and the task involved. It's important to know who you are interacting with and their preferred way of working. My personal preference in most situations is to know the end goal, see the big picture, and start from there.

But focusing on the end goal isn't always the right thing to do for me, and it isn't ever the right thing to do for some people. Sometimes, one step is all I want in the moment. For example, I know the end result of writing this book is that I want it published and out in the world. But at this moment, I need to stay focused on writing. Too many steps right now to my ultimate goal could confuse and overwhelm me. But if the task is to wash and dry the dishes, I can handle all the tools and directions at once.

To inspire others, we need to take the time to find out what they need and what inspires them, just as we need to regularly pause and ask ourselves what we need and what inspires us.

Set Them Up for Success

In supplying the right tools and the necessary information, we are setting others up for success. Sometimes this can be as simple as saying, "I need five red napkins from the basement cupboard, third shelf. Please get them and give them to Jeff. Let me know when he has them." That is specific, detailed, and clear. The person being asked to complete the task knows what is expected, and they will likely succeed.

Not everyone needs that much detail to help them succeed, though. Sometimes setting someone up to succeed might mean saying, "I need the room ready to go by 5:00 p.m. with tables set, food out, and servers ready. If you have any questions, please text me." Knowing who you are working with, their skill set, and their preferred way of being managed are key to giving them the tools they need to feel successful without feeling micromanaged.

Knowing how to do this well involves giving them the right amount of information. Too much will not motivate; neither will too little. And avoid withholding information. When we withhold information, it forces people to make things up, and that can sometimes be upsetting or even dangerous. Just think about the stories you make up when you haven't heard from someone. *She must be mad at me. Or maybe she's sick. Oh, no! Maybe she's been in an accident!* The mind goes looking for trouble where there may be none. Maybe she's just busy.

When we are open and forthcoming with what we are doing, others can follow more easily because their minds are not caught in trying to figure out what's coming next. This doesn't mean you have to provide every piece of information about a project or task, but sometimes we get stingy with sharing, either as a power play or just because we're busy and impatient. Withholding makes people feel excluded, and that is not a feeling that motivates! Sometimes we really have to stop and remember that people and relationships are ultimately what matters most.

Give the Relationship Precedence

Pay more attention to the relationship than the task. I promise, this is not counterproductive! When you take care of your relationships, the tasks take care of themselves. When you have the right team of people working towards a common goal, you have the potential for magic.

Many years ago, I was responsible for a team of about twenty running the kitchen for a retreat of 240. We were in a camp setting, so all groceries were being brought in by community members and being prepped on-site. It was a big job. Like many, I want things done in a certain way, and I often think that my certain way is the best way.

Near the beginning of the weekend, someone reminded me to just take care of the kitchen staff and not to worry about the tasks. At the time, this was challenging for me. But I did as instructed. I honestly don't remember doing much of anything that weekend except making sure the individuals on the kitchen crew were taken care of. We had music playing and massage breaks happening. I focused on asking everyone on the crew if they were okay instead of asking if the food was ready or the job was done.

Magic is the only way to describe what happened that weekend. Not only was the food on time and delicious, but everyone had fun. I was scratching my head at the end of the weekend, trying to figure out how it happened. I'd managed the kitchen for at least six other workshops where there was less to do and I'd worked much harder. This should have been the most labor intensive experience, but it felt effortless. I had a blast and so did everyone on my team.

This experience had a profound impact on me. Whenever I get caught up in trying to make sure someone else is doing the task according to my standards, I stop myself and remember my days managing the kitchen. And I remember what's important.

Fun, Fun, Fun

Fun is way too easily dismissed and way too important to not mention again. When you add a sway to your walk or a rhyme to your talk, life gets easier. Stress naturally dissolves. There are a million ways to add fun to any task that can enhance the work rather than distract from it. If you need some ideas, go back to Chapter 6 and review the list of ways to play I suggested.

Express Gratitude

Let others know you appreciate them. This is a simple but often overlooked way to connect with and inspire others. One of the key components of job satisfaction is feeling that your work is valued by others. Don't assume they know. The fact that they still have a job does not count as showing appreciation or value! Besides using words to express appreciation, take them out to lunch, buy them small gifts, and look at their vacation pictures. Pay attention to what they like to eat or read. Notice what music, hand lotion, or chewing gum they prefer.

According to authors Gary D. Chapman and Paul E. White, there are five primary love languages, and we each have our favorites. The languages are 1) words of affirmation, 2) spending quality time, 3) tangible gifts, 4) physical touch, and 5) acts of service.[19]

Whether you are trying to inspire an employee, a spouse, or a child, it makes sense to know what they respond to. Often, we know the love language of our cats and dogs better than anyone else in our lives. Who needs English?

Christine Caldwell once said that unexpressed gratitude, like any other unexpressed emotion, becomes a toxin in the body. When you naturally feel gratitude for someone else, move it out of your body. Get in the habit of expressing it to whomever you feel grateful.

Let Them Know They Make a Difference

One step beyond appreciation is letting others know how they have made a difference in your world or in the larger world. We all want to make a difference, and we all do. We just don't see how we do very often. When others tell us how even a smile transformed their day, we are moved and inspired to smile at someone else. One of my former clients is in the habit of saying, "Melanie fixed my brain," when she introduces me to others. I just have to think of her and I smile.

Play Break

Part 1: Make a list of the key players in your life, at home and at work. Allow yourself to imagine them gone and no one to fill their shoes. What would you miss?

Part 2: Tell them!

Fun, Fun, Fun

Oh, I already said that, didn't I?

Team Spirit

Often, team spirit becomes a command in the office and on the sports field instead of something that is created organically through interaction. The urging to get in the team spirit is used to manipulate and control, and for no good reason. The truth is that every person on the team, whether in the office or the field, is inherently important or they wouldn't have a position. Without the file clerk, all chaos would break loose. And who knows how many accidents are prevented by the person who operates the Zamboni machine?

Sometimes people don't act like team players because they are not treated as team players. Every job is a part of the whole, which makes every person automatically "on the team." It's the leader's job to know this and live the truth of it. That means everyone on the team is as important as everyone else. Sure, some people are easier to replace than others. But whoever is doing the job right now is important, and that's what matters. Or this could be you.

Be Irresistible

"Giving no reason to resist" is the essence of being irresistible. I heard this definition many years ago, but can't remember from whom. It is so to the point that it has stuck with me. When we interact with others without resistance, they feel it. It makes us very attractive and invites them to engage with us in the same way.

Be Impeccable

Stay in integrity with your values and what you speak to others. Lead by example and stay true to your heart. An unrecognized stressor is being out of alignment with yourself. You will feel it, and so will others. When you speak, make sure you believe what you are saying.

Taking the time to reflect on what inspires you does not have to be a big project. Use your daydreaming time to think about what you love and what makes you happy. Instead of paying attention to the worry thoughts, shift your awareness to the topic of inspiration. Keep a list handy for times when you forget. And most of all, don't make this another project to stress about.

Part III
Treatment Plans

9

Step-by-Step Guides to Handling Stress

We often read self-help books and feel excited about the great information and new ideas, but then continue on our merry (or not so merry) way without any significant changes in our approach to life. I have provided treatment plans based on common scenarios that can be stress inducing. My recommendation is to copy the pages, especially those that resonate with your situation(s), and keep them nearby. Next time you feel stressed, pull out your treatment plan instead of reaching for coffee or chocolate.

You will see the suggestion to let go many times throughout the treatment plans. Throughout this book, you have been practicing letting go by noticing thoughts, feelings, sensations, and reactions. You also practiced letting go by shaking your body. And you practiced letting go every time you laughed, and with every exhalation of your breath. If you still think you don't know how to let go, just pick up any object and drop it. If you can do that, you can let go. If you have resistance to letting go, ask yourself what you get from holding on. Or give yourself permission to hold on consciously for a certain period of time. Both of these alternatives will give you more information that may be necessary to fully let go.

Most of the suggestions can be done in thirty seconds or less, especially after you've practiced them for a while. And if they take longer than that, know that it is time well spent.

Stressor 1: Overwhelm

Presenting Issue/Symptoms: Too much to do, can't keep up, feeling overwhelmed.
Desired Outcome: Confidence in ability to handle all that is happening.
Therapeutic Interventions:

1. Breathe. Deeply inhale and fully exhale several times.
2. Allow yourself to feel as overwhelmed as you are, just for a moment. That means get conscious, stop what you are doing, and say to yourself, "Wow, I feel overwhelmed." Racing around and saying you are overwhelmed does not count as validating the feeling. Stop and acknowledge the feelings and the sensations. You will notice that your system begins to settle down and the upset begins to dissolve.
3. Notice your thoughts. What are you saying to yourself about yourself? Are those thoughts true? Are they helpful? See if you can find something to say that would be more supportive. For instance, you might say, "I have so much to do, it's a good thing I'm so competent."
4. Check your body posture. Are you sitting in a position that makes you feel you have the world on your shoulders? Try just dropping your shoulders and noticing that you aren't actually carrying anything on them. Try a different posture, or several. Try a different

chair when working at your desk. Ergonomic chairs or large balls force us into sitting up, which makes us feel more powerful.

5. If necessary, renegotiate agreements with yourself and others. If the demands are truly too great, first see who they are coming from: you or someone else. If they are coming from someone else, talk to that person and ask which are their highest priorities and what do they need done first, letting them know (as calmly as possible), that getting it all done is not humanly possible within the currently established timeframe. If you are putting the demands on yourself, have the same conversation with yourself. Stop and prioritize.
6. Schedule play breaks—this can be as simple as thirty seconds with a windup toy—or find a way to have fun with what you are doing.
7. Embrace the feeling of overwhelm. As best you can, make friends with the feeling and know it won't kill you.

Stressor 2: Relationships

Presenting Issue/Symptoms: My coworkers are incompetent. At least it seems that way.

Desired Outcome: Imperturbability, calm and unruffled self-assurance or equanimity, steadiness of mind.

Therapeutic Interventions:

1. Breathe. Deeply inhale and fully exhale several times.
2. Pause for a moment and ask yourself how their incompetence impacts you.

   If it really *doesn't* affect you, just let it go. Notice that you don't have to react to them. Ask yourself,

"Do I really want to spend my energy on this?" or "Do I want to let this control me?" With another deep breath, you can imagine dropping the upset you've been carrying.

If it *does* affect you in terms of having to correct their mistakes or redo something, allow yourself to think about doing so and notice what feelings arise.

If it brings up overwhelm, go back to Stressor 1 and follow the suggested activities.

If it brings up anger, feel the sensations in your body and check to see if there is some action you need to take (such as alerting a supervisor). If there is no action to be taken, see what's driving the anger. Under the anger there could be a desire to control them or want them to be different than the way they are, a desire for approval, a desire for job security, a desire for everyone to get along, or a desire to get away from the situation. As you notice what underlies the anger, you can now acknowledge the feeling at a deeper level and then choose whether or not you need to stay angry.

3. Physically remove yourself from the situation when possible. If you hate the way Sue answers the phone, move to where you can't hear her. If Joe comes in every day after lunch smelling of tobacco and you hate that smell, plan on doing a task that takes you out of the area for a few minutes.
4. Imagine the offending person(s) as a five-year-old who was never taught how to be in the world. Try to get in touch with the part of yourself that is a natural teacher or parent and gently teach them what you know.

5. Check the projection! Is there something you see in them that you can't tolerate in yourself? If so, acknowledge it and as best you can, love yourself even with your alleged shortcomings.

Stressor 3: Irritability

Presenting Issue/Symptoms: Every little thing is annoying.
Desired Outcome: Internal calm.
Therapeutic Interventions:

1. Awareness. The first step in creating a shift in a pattern (short-term or long-term) is to begin to recognize it as it is happening. Pay attention to when during the day you are most irritable, what things appear to set you off, and how you deal with the feelings. Do you take your feelings out on others or do you internalize them?
2. Become aware of the physical sensations that accompany irritation. I have felt the stir of irritation as a tingling in my arms, but you may feel it in your stomach, your shoulders, or your throat. Your body will register the irritation even before your mind does.
3. Curiosity. Allow yourself to wonder what is going on with you. How long have you been feeling this way? Were there obvious precipitating factors like a missed meal, change in diet, drinking or smoking cessation, or new coworkers?
4. Read through the other stressors in this section. Is your irritability connected to taking on too much, saying yes when you want to say no, physical pain and discomfort, or any other of the mentioned situations?

5. Are you using irritability to create distance or a boundary? Though it can be an effective barrier to keep others away, you are the one living with the discomfort of being irritable. There are better ways to get some space. (See the treatment plan for stressor 4.)
6. Take ownership. What action steps do you need to take to move out of the irritability? Here are some possibilities:
    - sleep more
    - cut sugar and alcohol from your diet
    - have your hormone levels checked
    - decrease caffeine consumption
    - eat more often
    - take more time for yourself
    - get professional help

Stressor 4: Too Many Demands

Presenting Issue/Symptoms: Everybody wants something from you; no time to yourself.

Desired Outcome: Putting yourself higher on the priority list, and/or saying no more often.

Therapeutic Interventions (for putting yourself higher on the priority list):

1. Make a list of all the areas in your life that you manage. This is fun to do on a mind map. (Visit www.mindmapping.com.)
2. What is more important than you? Notice how it feels in your body to be less important. What's the body posture that goes with feeling less important? Notice how the body posture would shift if you were just as

important or more important than whatever you identified. Experience this new posture for thirty seconds.

3. Do an honest evaluation of your priorities.
4. Assess how much time you spent working, resting, playing, and taking time for yourself.
5. Determine what an ideal ratio would be.
6. Journal or list what action steps you could take to achieve balance.
7. Commit to taking one small step in that direction.

Therapeutic Interventions (for saying no more often):

1. Think about saying no in a situation where it feels challenging to do that.
2. Notice what images come to mind when you think about saying no, what sensations you feel in your body, and any thoughts or beliefs you have about saying no. Be willing to allow any uncomfortable memories to arise.
3. Find the posture of no in your body. If you notice you are shrinking or contracting, try on a bigger, more firm no. Notice if you enjoy it or feel a little frightened by it. Either way, keep practicing.
4. Practice saying no in areas that are less uncomfortable and build up to the more difficult ones.
5. Think of a friend who is really good at saying no and imagine being him or her in those tough situations.
6. Play with saying the words "yes" and "no" for as long as it takes to notice they are both just sounds.
7. Imagine your inner child saying, "No, no, no," as she stamps her foot and throws a fit.

8. Don't look for excuses. Just say no. The more you feel you have to defend your no, the more it will feel wrong that you are saying it.
9. Remember that you have now put yourself higher on the priority list and if you say yes to others, you are saying no to yourself.

Stressor 5: Guilty of Inappropriate Behavior

Presenting Issue/Symptoms: Stress got the better of you and you took it out on others.
Desired Outcome: Ability to hold your head up.
Therapeutic Interventions:

1. Breathe. Deeply inhale and fully exhale several times. (Yes, back to the breath.)
2. Are you trying to justify, defend, and explain your behavior, even to yourself? If so, stop it. It won't work and it will keep you caught in the spin of feeling bad.
3. Admit to yourself that you acted in a way that you don't feel proud of. Allow yourself to feel any feelings that get stirred up including regret, sadness, or anger.
4. If you're punishing yourself—telling yourself how bad and wrong you were—for the behavior, ask yourself this question: How long and/or how much do I deserve to be punished? You may be able to decide that you've done enough already or that you need to continue for another hour or day. See what you think you'll get from punishing yourself. If you think that it will prevent you from ever doing that behavior again, know that it won't work. You're just giving more attention to the behavior

that you don't want, increasing the probability of it happening again.

5. Apologize, sincerely and without excuses.
6. Move on.

Stressor 6: Lack of Appreciation

Presenting Issue/Symptoms: You work your butt off and nobody seems to notice or say thank you.
Desired Outcome: Feeling appreciated.
Therapeutic Interventions:

1. Check in with yourself and see if it's really true that you are not being appreciated. When we can't appreciate ourselves, it can sometimes be hard to feel appreciated by others. So before going to Step 2, just notice if you may be overlooking existing displays of gratitude.
2. If there really is a lack of expression, the next question to ask yourself is whether others know what or how much you are doing. If they don't, how can you (your adult self, that is) let them know?
3. Make a list of the ways you would like to be appreciated. When possible, let others know how much you appreciate being appreciated.
4. Remember how great you are! When we have the ability to appreciate ourselves, all external gratitude is superfluous. Get in the practice of saying, "Good job! Way to go!" to yourself. Take it in and absorb it.

Stressor 7: Lack of Respect, Scenario A

Presenting Issue/Symptoms: Employees take advantage of you; people speak over you or down to you.

Desired Outcome: Respect.

Therapeutic Interventions:

1. Breathe. Deeply inhale and fully exhale several times.
2. Mentally acknowledge that someone is being rude or disrespectful and you feel hurt. This will stop you from going into a full-blown reaction, which could be either taking in and swallowing their behavior, or screaming at them.
3. Have an internal conversation with yourself along these lines: *Wow. I can't believe how rude this person is. Didn't anybody teach them any manners? Or, Huh, look at that, Joe is being a jerk again!* Or, *I wonder how Emily missed etiquette school?* Again, these internal dialogues will help you get some distance from your reactive self.
4. In the moment, shift your body position. According to the practice of aikido, a Japanese martial art, if you are facing the person straight on, you are more vulnerable to attack. Turn your body on the diagonal and imagine your body deflecting their words. Let the words soar past you.
5. Consider whether you need to take action or just let go. If you know the comments are not personal, that this person acts this way with everyone in their life (and they are not your child), I suggest letting it go. We don't need to take on everyone's bad behavior. If it's only you they are disrespectful towards, you will need to take some action.
6. Possible actions include:
   a. walking away every time you are treated badly
   b. speaking up so you are noticed

c. firing the employee
d. quitting your job
e. talking to a supervisor
f. gently pushing back (Often people are just seeing how far we can be pushed.)
g. imagining what you might do to this person if there were no consequence (Don't hold back. Have fun with this. Tar and feather them, publicly humiliate them, or kick and punch them. This will help move the anger from your body. It is not a dress rehearsal or warm-up. When you let yourself do what you really want to do, in your mind's eye, it will move the stuck energy from your body and eliminate the need to act out.)

Stressor 8: Lack of Respect, Scenario B

Presenting Issue/Symptoms: A friend, loved one, or coworker makes constant digs, sometimes adding that they are just joking or having fun with you.
Desired Outcome: Respect.
Therapeutic Interventions:

1. Smack them upside the head. Yes, I'm kidding! But I wanted you to know that the desire to do so is an appropriate mental and emotional reaction to this type of behavior.
2. If you are in the habit of defending yourself, stop it. You're wasting your time and you will just give more energy to what you don't want.
3. Tell them, "Stop it!
4. Tell them again!

5. And, again.
6. These types of digs can fall into the definition of verbal abuse or harassment. People often don't recognize how hurtful their comments can be and truly believe they are just playing with you. Don't worry about being a poor sport. This is not a fun game for anyone (even the attacker), and no one walks away the winner.

Stressor 9: Lousy Environment

Presenting Issue/Symptoms: Everybody you work with is miserable all the time and constantly complaining.
Desired Outcome: Joy.
Therapeutic Interventions:

1. Let them be miserable. Trying to change the attitudes of others by encouraging them to look on the positive side is rarely effective.
2. Don't join them. Though it may appear attractive to commiserate with them and tell your own stories of woe, it won't make you feel any better and will likely bring you down. The game of "Can You Top This?" is not worth playing when it comes to suffering. Misery doesn't really love company.
3. Imagine the complainers as three-year-olds.
4. Disarm them. Compliment them on what they're wearing, tell them about the great lunch spot you just found, start laughing about something you just remembered, and share the humor with them.
5. Remember that misery is not like the measles; it's not contagious. When you become afraid of "catching the negativity," you're giving it energy and pulling it

towards you. And if you start complaining about the complainers, they've sucked you in.

Stressor 10: Holding on to Past Grievances, Scenario A

Presenting Issue/Symptoms: You were hurt by someone in the past and can't forgive; you are feeling resentful.

Desired Outcome: Peace.

Therapeutic Interventions:

1. Remind yourself that the anger is in your body and you are the one suffering because of it. Nobody else feels it to the degree you do.
2. Assuming you have tried to let it go and don't feel like you can, ask yourself what you get from holding on to the anger. Sometimes we think anger protects us from making another stupid mistake or from being hurt again by that person or anyone else. Sometimes we think they deserve our wrath for the rest of their lives. If you remember that you are the one feeling that anger in your body, you will see that by not forgiving, you are pretty much giving that person permission to hurt you for the rest of your life, not the other way around.
3. See if there is some action you haven't taken that prevents the anger from letting go. Anger is a way of informing us that we've been wronged. Do you need to pursue charges, change the locks on your doors, or write a letter?
4. Check to see if beneath the anger at the other person, you are really angry at yourself. If so, what would it take to forgive yourself?

Stressor 11: Holding on to Past Grievances, Scenario B

Presenting Issue/Symptoms: You are angry at yourself for hurting another or for allowing yourself to be hurt.

Desired Outcome: Peace.

Therapeutic Interventions:

1. Ask yourself, honestly, "Why did that happen?" It is almost always true that we are doing the best we can with what we know. Most of the time we judge ourselves as if we had more information in the past than we actually did.
2. Again, ask yourself, honestly, "Will I ever do that again?" Almost always, the answer to this question is, "No way." If you know this for a fact, you will see that you don't need to hold on to the anger to prevent yourself from doing that again.
3. Then decide if you have punished yourself enough. If the answer is yes, just let it go. If the answer is no, come up with a plan for how and when you will complete the punishment and be done with it.
4. If someone else had made the same mistake, would you still be angry with them? Almost always, we are hardest on ourselves.
5. Every time you hear the internal voice saying that you messed up, make a song or rhyme out of it. For example, if you are blaming yourself for your lousy judge of character, try singing to the tune of "Mary Had a Little Lamb," these words: "Susie had a slip of mind, slip of mind, slip of mind. Susie had a slip of mind and it cost her three long years." Then let it go.

Stressor 12: Physical Pain or Discomfort

Presenting Issue/Symptoms: Your body hurts!

Desired Outcome: Relief from suffering.

Therapeutic Interventions:

1. Practice loving-kindness. We often judge ourselves for our pain and/or illness. When we are blamed by others or blame ourselves, we contract in reaction. Contraction closes in on pain and makes it worse. Remember that you are a human being having a human experience, and you are doing the best you can with what you have available in the moment.
2. Pay attention! Pain can be an indicator that something is amiss. Get curious about your pain. Is it warning you about a serious imbalance in your system? Is it letting you know something about someone or something in your environment? Keep in mind that when we ignore our pain, it often escalates, much like a child wanting to be noticed.
3. Breathe. Breath works hand in hand with attention. When we breathe into a sensation, we are giving it attention. But we are also validating it, saying it is worthy of our energy. Also, breathing expands the area around the pain by providing oxygen and space. Letting the pain get bigger is a meditation technique that works with breath to expand the area the pain takes. While this may be a frightening thought, think about liquid on a surface: the larger the surface, the thinner the consistency of the fluid. When pain is spread out over a larger area, it becomes less intense.

4. Let go of wanting to change it. A very simple and powerful thing you can do is ask yourself, "Could I let go of wanting to change this?" Our resistance to the pain actually keeps it locked in place, and willingness to be with it may give it space enough to shift.
5. Be willing to take a sick day if necessary to take care of yourself.

Stressor 13: Financially Stretched

Presenting Issue/Symptoms: It feels like there's not enough; it always feels tight.
Desired Outcome: Be at peace with finances.
Therapeutic Interventions:

1. Accurately assess the situation. Are finances as tight as you think or are you just in the habit of saying that there's not enough?
2. If, in fact, there is enough, stop saying there isn't.
3. Notice the tightness in your body when you start talking about money. Try to relax the muscles and open inside. Remember, where the body goes, the mind will follow.
4. Instead of using the words, "I can't afford it," try, "It's not where I want to spend my money."
5. Make up rhymes and songs to familiar tunes about the ease you have with money. (My favorite is, "The money in the bank goes up, up, up" to the tune of "The Wheels on the Bus.")
6. If you spend money to handle feelings, identify at least three things you could do instead of shop.

7. Take action steps to change your situation if necessary, including creating and following a budget, exploring options for more income and less expenses, and/or getting professional help. Let yourself get creative with this. Ask yourself questions like, "What's the wildest way I could get more money?" or "What's the simplest way to have more money?"
8. Imagine the people you know with an abundance of money (including famous people you've never met) brainstorming with you about your situation. Listen to what they have to say.

Stressor 14: Change, Scenario A

Presenting Issue/Symptoms: You've just moved to a new home or new job.
Desired Outcome: Flexibility.
Therapeutic Interventions:

1. Breathe. Deeply inhale and fully exhale several times. (Yes, again.)
2. Acknowledge to yourself that change is challenging for most people and it is okay if you're uncomfortable for a while.
3. Give yourself time to find your rhythm in your new situation.
4. You may be feeling "out of step" or "out of rhythm" in your life. If so, dance breaks may help you find your rhythm again.
5. Don't expect to be perfect or know everything the first day. Be willing to ask for help.

6. Create at least one small area for yourself with personal items. At work, it may just be a couple of pictures in a drawer. At home, if you don't have a room to yourself, set up a chair and altar with items meaningful to you. Knowing there's a personal haven helps during transitions.
7. Give yourself some approval for having the courage to make the changes you are making. No one likes change because it requires more learning and effort than we are accustomed to.

Stressor 15: Change, Scenario B

Presenting Issue/Symptoms: Your best friend at work is leaving, your children are going off to college, or someone you've depended on has died.

Desired Outcome: Peace.

Therapeutic Interventions:

1. Whatever the situation, acknowledge that you are grieving. Trying to rationalize or "buck up" doesn't work.
2. Notice the things you are saying to yourself about the loss. If you are telling yourself that you can't live without them, that there is no one to turn to, or saying anything else that constitutes hyperbole, check and see what's really true.
3. Now write out the things that are hardest for you about the loss. What may be accurate is that your life will change without them, you will have to find new friends, and you will miss them.
4. Create a plan to keep the connection alive. That may

be weekly phone calls, daily e-mails, or visits to a gravesite. Know that you can also call upon the deceased in your own mind by asking what he or she would tell you in that moment. Journaling is another way of communicating.

5. Remember the things you do on a daily basis that you learned from that person. This is one way of honoring their memory.

Stressor 16: Change, Scenario C

Presenting Issue/Symptoms: You are getting divorced or a loved one has died.

Desired Outcome: Having the ability to move through and experience grief and still function in the world.

Therapeutic Interventions:

1. As with stressor 15, you are grieving, but at a more intense level. All the interventions previously suggested still apply, plus a few more.
2. Know that grieving comes in waves and has a cycle of its own that is unique to you. Some days you may feel like crying, other days you may feel angry or numb. Let go of trying to figure out why you feel the way you do at any given moment.
3. Let the grief take as long as it does. As a general rule, society does not know what to do with those grieving and wants the experience to go away quickly. It's not uncommon for others to expect you to get over it much faster than you do.
4. If you need to work while grieving, continue to acknowledge the feelings throughout your day, as

best you can. You can feel sensation without falling apart.

5. Dance your grief with others or by yourself. The body is brilliant at moving through feelings when we let it move uncensored. Your dance doesn't have to look good. Knowing that grief moves in waves—some gentle, some strong—imagine waves moving through your body.
6. In the case of a divorce, remember that you are also grieving the dream of a long, happy life together. Even when we know divorce is best, the dreams we had about the relationship are gone now, too. Often, this is where the real heartbreak is.

Stressor 17: Self-Doubt

Presenting Issue/Symptoms: You feel incapable of meeting the task at hand.

Desired Outcome: Grace under pressure.

Therapeutic Interventions:

1. Breathe. Deeply inhale and fully exhale several times.
2. Assess the situation. What aspect of it is most daunting?
3. Take an inventory: Is this something you've done before? Is it similar to anything you've ever done before? Is there a manual? Who do you know that knows how to do this?
4. Acknowledge the internal voices that may be saying you don't know what you're doing. For instance, thank them and tell them that what they are saying

isn't helpful at the moment. Ask them what else they've got.

5. Play with movements that convey the message, "I don't know what I'm doing." (Just don't do it in front of your supervisor.) Physically moving the feeling in your body will help you get out of the fear of being stuck.
6. If appropriate, remind yourself that you are capable and can figure it out.
7. If you can't do it on your own, get help.
8. After it's done, give yourself some praise. You deserve it.

Stressor 18: Excessive Worry

Presenting Issue/Symptoms: Habitual worrying even when things are going well.

Desired Outcome: Freedom from the worry habit.

Therapeutic Interventions:

1. Revisit Chapter 3, which deals with the habit of worry.
2. Remind yourself that you are capable and can deal with circumstances as they arise. (Worrying is sending the opposite message.)
3. Hold in mind what you really want to have happen, not the picture that goes with worrying.
4. Feel any associated feelings of fear, sadness, or anger and let them move through you.
5. If you're worrying as a strategy to remember to do something, buy a new pen and pad just for these kinds of things or learn how to use your mobile phone reminders.

6. Throw a worry party for yourself.
7. If everyone in your family worries, let go of wanting to be like them.
8. Embody the character of The Worrywart or The Mad Hatter and have fun with it.

Stressor 19: Nagging Critical Voice

Presenting Issue/Symptoms: A voice in your head is often telling you that you are doing it wrong, not good enough, not smart enough, etc.
Desired Outcome: Support from the internal voices.
Therapeutic Interventions:

1. Revisit Chapter 1 about dealing with intrusive thoughts.
2. Remember that you don't have to listen to or believe everything you think.
3. Imagine those voices sitting on the couch next to you instead of coming from within. Would you sit there and listen or get up and leave?
4. Turn your inner critic into your inner coach. Acknowledge that there may be something important in the feedback, but the message is not being delivered very effectively. See the habits chapter for dealing with this.
5. Notice if the voice sounds like someone from your past (typically Mom or Dad). Knowing that the words are just a repeat of past patterns can help you get some distance.
6. Turn the words into a song. It's amazing how

"You don't know what you're doing" can transform when sung to "I'm a Little Teacup."

7. Declare that only the internal voice that is your highest and best supporter can have the floor for the next thirty seconds. If the critics return after thirty seconds, again call on the highest and best supporter to speak up.

Stressor 20: You Can't Get What You Want

Presenting Issue/Symptoms: You feel defeated.

Desired Outcome: Peace.

Therapeutic Interventions:

1. Ask yourself what beliefs accompany defeat. Do you believe you are being persecuted? That you are not trying hard enough? That it's just not meant to be?
2. Challenge those beliefs with these questions: "What do I get from believing that?" "What would happen if I didn't believe that?"
3. Allow yourself to feel what defeated feels like in your body.
4. Do a defeated dance.
5. Notice if feelings of anger, apathy, lust, fear, grief, or pride are attached to defeat. If so, be with the sensations that accompany each feeling.
6. Do another dance with the feelings that you identified.
7. Draw the feeling.
8. If the experience of defeat is premature, give yourself permission to postpone feeling it until you know for sure.

9. Allow your internal optimist to have a heart-to-heart with your internal pessimist. Be sure to give them equal floor time.
10. Give yourself permission to give up for an hour, a day, or a week.
11. Do an honest assessment about the pros and cons of having what you desire.

Okay, I've gotten you started with generic treatment plans. Now it's your turn. Take these plans and highlight them, add to them, and delete from them in any way that serves you. Practice different strategies and choose your favorites. Some will only work sometimes. Others will be really powerful in one situation, but not in another. Do what works. There is no right or wrong.

10

Conclusion

Life can be challenging. You may encounter more roadblocks and upsets than you bargained for. Some days may be miserable; some days you may feel like giving up. On those days, I hope you allow yourself to feel your feelings fully, for a little while anyway.

It's also true that life can be fun. You can be happy. You can live without stress. If you want to. It's not required. Our natural state is full of peace and joy, but it is often covered up with thoughts and feelings that don't support well-being.

Learning to be just a little irreverent means recognizing that all the things we think are so important might not be. Being a little irreverent asks that we take life just a bit less seriously and embrace having fun, even with our thoughts and feelings.

I have given you many tools and techniques that take little or no time to implement. But they do take commitment and persistence. Doing any of them once or twice may provide relief temporarily. But consistently practicing them will change how you perceive the world, which ultimately determines your stress level and how much you enjoy life.

Can you give yourself the 30-second play breaks that can change your life?

About the Author

Melanie Smithson was always the one that was a little too happy, a little too optimistic, and maybe just a little too full of herself. Once upon a time, she may have tried to curb that. No more. Now she is the one who embraces too happy, too optimistic, and too full of herself. Is there anything better to be full of?

Melanie has journeyed through her share of grief and stress and has lived to tell the tale. Dragged to her first dance class at the age of four, the power of movement and the wisdom of the body are in her bones (and muscles, fluids, nervous system). The traditional and nontraditional trainings from Naropa University, Sedona Method Associates, The Newton Organization, and Intuitive Advantage have bestowed upon her the titles of Licensed Professional Counselor, Board Certified Dance Movement Therapist, Certified Sedona Method Coach, Certified Hypnotherapist, and Master of Arts. Earning each molded and shaped who she is and how she perceives the world. And they have given her many modalities to play with in her life and psychotherapy practice.

She is co-owner of Smithson Clinic, Inc. (www.smithson-clinic.com) with her husband, Gail, in Denver, Colorado, where they live with their supreme playmate, the four-legged Beatrice.

Melanie offers workshops and trainings throughout the world. To learn more about these, visit www.melaniesmithson.com.

More Information

The author, Melanie Smithson, is available for speaking engagements, keynote addresses, teaching workshops, seminars, breakout sessions, events, and industry-specific trainings. Melanie is an engaging facilitator able to effectively motivate and move audiences. Participants can immediately employ the tools offered to reduce stress and embrace joy. Burnout rates go down, productivity goes up, and the world becomes a happier place. For information or booking inquiries, please call 303-271-7659 or send an email to speaker@melaniesmithson.com. Melanie is also available for a limited number of private consultations.

Free Gift from the Author

As a very special thank-you for purchasing this book, Melanie has a free gift for you. Continue your commitment to stress free living with your own personalized Action Plan. Go to www.melaniesmithson.com/stressfreeplan and download the template today.

Bonus Gift: Your Own Personalized Treatment Plan

Like the treatment plans in the book? Have a specific situation in your life that you need a personalized plan for? Go to www.melaniesmithson.com to submit your request and Melanie will write a plan just for you.

Notes

1. Susan Aposhyan, *Natural Intelligence: Body-Mind Integration and Human Development* (Baltimore: Lippincott Williams & Wilkins, 1999), 66.

2. Dr. Frederic Luskin, PhD, *Forgive for Good: A Proven Prescription for Health and Happiness* (New York: Harper Collins, 2003).

3. Bre Pettis and Kio Stark, http://www.brepettis.com/blog/2009/3/3/the-cult-of-done-manifesto.html.

4. Judith L. Rapoport, *The Boy Who Couldn't Stop Washing*, (New York: Signet, 1991).

5. Mihaly Csikszentmihalyi, *Finding Flow* (New York: Basic Books, 1997).

6. Hale Dwoskin, *The Sedona Method Seminar Notes*, (Sedona, Arizona, 2006 – 2013).

7. A.J. Deikman, *The Observing Self*, Beacon Press, Boston, 1982.

8. Howard Markman, *Fighting for Your Marriage*, John Wiley and Sons, NJ, 1994.

9. T.W. Pace, PhD, LT Negi, PhD, D. D. Adame, et al. "Effect of Compassion Meditation on Neuroendocrine, Innate Immune and Behavioral Responses to Psychosocial Stress," *Psychoneuroendocrinology*, 2009; 34(1), 87 – 98.

10. Marc Bangert, and Eckart O Altenmüller, "Mapping Perception to Action in Piano Practice: A Longitudinal DC-EEG Study," *BMC Neuroscience*, 2003, 4:26.

11. Mihaly Csikszentmihalyi, *Flow*, (New York: Harper & Row, 1990).

12. Brian Sutton Smith, PhD, *The Ambiguity of Play*, (Boston: Harvard University Press, 1997).

13. Alexander Lowen, MD, *The Voice of the Body*, Selected Public Lectures 1962 – 1982, (Vermont: The Alexander Lowen Foundation, 2005).

14. Joseph Heller, *Bodywise*, (California: North Atlantic Books, 1986).

15. Stanley Keleman, *Your Body Speaks Its Mind*, (California: Center Press, 1975).

16. Amy Cuddy, "Your Body Language Shapes Who You Are," *Ted Talk*, (2012).

17. http://newsfeed.time.com/2013/03/25/more-people-have-cell-phones-than-toilets-u-n-study-shows/

18. R. B. Zajonc, "Styles of explanation in social psychology," *European Journal of Social Psychology*, 19(5), 1989. 345 – 368.

19. Gary Chapman and Paul White, *The 5 Languages of Appreciation in the Workplace: Empowering Organizations by Encouraging People*, (Illinois: Northfield Publishing, 2010).

Recommended Resources

Books

Attwood, Janet Bray and Chris. *The Passion Test.* New York: 8Hudson Street Press, 2007.

Borich, Judy. *Touch and Go: The Nature of Intimacy.* Tijeras, New Mexico: Interact Publishing, 2002.

Brown, MD, Stuart and Vaughan, Christopher. Play: *How it Shapes the Brain, Opens the Imagination, and Invigorates the Soul,* New York: Penguin Group, 2009.

Caldwell, Christine. *Getting Our Bodies Back.* Boston, Massachusetts: Shambala Publications, 1996.

Canfield, Jack, and Switzer, Janet. *The Success Principles.* New York: HarperCollins Publishers, 2005.

Csikszentmihaly, Mihaly. *Flow: The Psychology of Optimal Experience.* New York: Harper & Row Publishers, Inc., 1990.

Deikman, Arthur. *The Observing Self.* Boston, Massachusetts: Beacon Press, 1982.

Donaldson, Fred. *Playing by Heart.* Deerfield Beach, Florida: Health Communications, Inc., 1993.

Dwoskin, Hale. *The Sedona Method.* Sedona, Arizona: Sedona Press, 2003.

Foster, Jeff. *An Extraordinary Absence: Liberation in the Midst of a Very Ordinary Life.* Salisbury, UK: Non-Duality Press, 2009.

Keleman, Stanley. *Your Body Speaks Its Mind.* Berkeley, California: Center Press, 1975.

Levy, Fran. *Dance Movement Therapy: A Healing Art.* Reston, Virginia: The American Alliance for Health, Physical Education, Recreation, and Dance, 1988.

Lowen, Alexander. *The Spirituality of the Body.* New York: MacMillan Publishing Co., 1990.

McGonigal, Phd, Kelly. *The Willpower Instinct: How Self-Control Works, Why It Matters, and What You Can Do to Get More of It.* New York: Penguin Group, 2012.

Nachmanovitc, Stephen. *Free Play: The Power of Improvisation in Life and the Arts.* New York: G.P. Putnam's Sons, 1990.

Phillips, Jan. *The Art of Original Thinking.* San Diego, California: 9th Element Press, 2006.

Roth, Gabrielle. *Maps to Ecstasy: The Healing Power of Movement.* Novato, California: Natraj Publishing, 1998.

Singer, Michael A. *The Untethered Soul.* Oakland, California: New Harbinger Publications, Inc., 2007.

Trainings, Seminars, and Audio Programs

The Sedona Method, Audio recordings, books, retreats and trainings, www.Sedona.com

Breakthrough to Success Training, www.canfieldtrainings.com

Sacred Living Workshops with Judy Borich, Jborich@aol.com, 505-266-1500

Soma: Move and Be Moved, Movement journeys with Jessica Morningstar Wolf, www.facebook.com/somagypsy, www.jessicamorningstarwolf.com

Gabrielle Roth's 5 Rhythms, http://www.5rhythms.com/

MA Program in Somatic Counseling Psychology, Naropa University, Boulder, Colorado, www.naropa.edu/academics/gsp/grad/somatic-counseling-psychology-ma/